Ordnance

Oxf...

CITY WALKS

Compiled by
Victoria Bentata Azaz

Victoria Bentata Azaz is an Oxford graduate,
a locally based Green Badge Guide and a
member of the Oxford Guild of Guides.

 # Contents

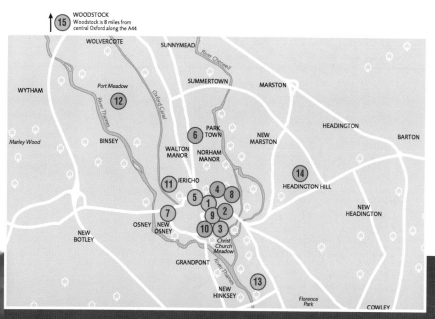

Tales for the telling en route

Tales for the telling en route	Page
Magnificently imposing buildings and impeccably maintained quads, a curious college founding, the Oxford Emperors and the 'Angel of Broad Street', ceremony, tradition and film locations. Quintessential Oxford.	6
A taste of literary Oxford from Lewis Carroll to William Golding and Shelley to Tolkien. Plus the Bodleian's treasures, Blackwell's literary associations aplenty from Harry Potter to Inspector Morse.	12
Trade in corn, meat and fish and the 'new' Covered Market; the oldest building in Oxford, two fine old inns, Carfax Tower, Oxford's worst riots, England's first hot air balloonist and views from Christ Church Meadow.	18
Pre-Raphaelite art and beautiful architecture, carvings in stone and wood, Edmond Halley and William Spooner, the old East Gate, the oldest purpose-built concert hall and, perhaps, try a yard of ale at The Turf?	24
So much absorbing history in the bloody past of Oxford's castle and prison, and in the treasures of three world-class museums. For lighter diversions take in the arts venues and literary inspiration at two city pubs.	30
A tour of the smart Victorian suburbs of North Oxford charting the rise of former women-only colleges; the original Radcliffe Infirmary, the Dragon School and the pillar box built for the editor of the OED.	36
Drinking ale was often safer than water in medieval times and the abbeys and colleges all had brewhouses so merchants, brewers and friars lived side by side in Osney. Frank Cooper's marmalade came much later.	42
Tales of scientific endeavour through thrifty experimentation and generous philanthropy - anatomists, botanists, chemists and philosophers have brought great medical advances and a clutch of Nobel Prizes.	48
A doctor who avoided sick patients, eminent neurosurgeons, the motorcycle crash helmet, a woman raised from the dead, royal physicians and the 17th century apothecaries. Plus a tour of Christ Church.	54
Dating back to Norman times, Oxford has a rich Jewish history: from housing the king's crossbowmen to England's first coffee house and Frideswide's revenge to Albert Einstein and other notable refugee scholars.	60
Lined with attractive houseboats, the canal once brought coal to the city's industries in Jericho, now a quieter setting for a grand church, synagogue, cemetery and unique doorway carvings of Elijah the Prophet.	66
A circuit of Port Meadow – a 1,000-year old pasture with views of the 'dreaming spires', pioneering aviators, Alice's Treacle Well, King Henry II's mistress at Godstow Abbey and King Charles I's retreat from Cromwell.	72
College rowing and all manner of other boating activities, pastoral riverside and waterside wildlife, the beautiful Norman church in Iffley village, a celebrated foodie pub and record-breaking athletic endeavour.	78
Walking parts of the old routeway, Cuckoo Lane is traced from attractive Old Headington to the tranquil River Cherwell and along Mesopotamia Walk to the wooded parkland of the University Parks.	84
Fine old coaching inns and distinguished, characterful buildings make Woodstock an historic delight and only a short stroll from the splendours of Blenheim Palace and its classic English parkland setting.	90

Introduction to City Walks Oxford

Oxford is the perfect city for walkers. Indeed, so packed is this compact city with architectural and historical treasures, gardens, river walks, narrow lanes and exhibition spaces that it simply cannot properly be explored any other way.

On foot, you can enter the colleges and museums, walk in the University Parks and Christ Church Meadow, picnic by the rivers Isis and Cherwell and climb to the top of the city's highest towers to enjoy some spectacular views of Oxford's busy streets, 'dreaming spires', libraries and University buildings. You can also stop to look skywards and admire the thousands of stone carvings, exquisite grotesques and gargoyles which adorn its buildings.

A visit to coincide with an Oxford celebration brings additional ceremonial spectacle. Listen to the choir at Magdalen Tower at dawn on May Morning (1st May) or see the pageantry of

Carfax Tower

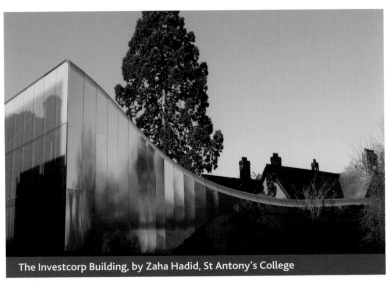

The Investcorp Building, by Zaha Hadid, St Antony's College

a University procession at Encaenia, where honorary degrees are awarded on Wednesday of the 9th week of Trinity (summer) term.

Oxford's manifold treasures are on open display to any passing pedestrian, but this book brings them to life. Route commentaries provide factual information, anecdotal tales and wonderfully quirky details. Its 15 walks take you to some of Oxford's suburbs and villages –

Blavatnik School of Government

individual colleges and schools, the Civil War, the medieval Jewish community... Find King Richard the Lionheart's birthplace, Sir Christopher Wren's first masterpiece, the site of the earliest coffee house in England, and read hidden stone codes.

For even greater depth, book a qualified Blue or Green Badge guide either privately or at the city's Visitor Information Centre on Broad Street.

Happy walking!

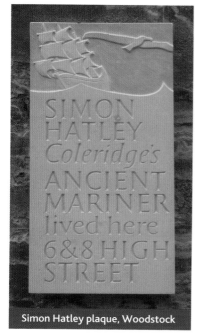
Simon Hatley plaque, Woodstock

Jericho, Osney, Wolvercote, Binsey, Headington and Iffley and an outlier – a walk round lovely Woodstock and Blenheim Palace's park. However, Oxford itself remains at the heart of the book, with its world renowned university and extraordinary college system, its myriad royal connections and the amazing creativity of its citizens and academics, who have given us everything from the Morris Minor to marmalade and antibiotics to Alice in Wonderland. The rationale for the routes is in some cases geographical, but in many cases it is tied to a particular story: scientific and medical developments, great literature, art and architecture, sport, religion, women, publishing,

Bodleian Library

The Broad to the High

WALK 1

An old Oxford joke features a tourist who asks for directions to the University, only to be told that it is 'everywhere'. Indeed, there is no central campus and its buildings are scattered liberally around the city. Nevertheless, the most magnificent and important are undoubtedly concentrated in the small area covered by this walk. As distinguished architectural historian Nikolaus Pevsner aptly put it, 'There is a density of monuments of architecture here which has not the like in Europe'.

Start	Finish	Distance	Refreshments
Visitor Information Centre, Broad Street	The Buttery, Broad Street	¾ mile (1.2km)	The Buttery

The Sheldonian Theatre

ON THIS WALK

	Balliol College	Trinity College	Line of carvings
🚶	'The Angel of Broad Street'	Sheldonian Theatre	Bridge of Sighs

Begin at the **Visitor Information Centre**, on Broad Street.

Look across the road to the imposing façade of **Balliol College**, one of the oldest of the 38 colleges of the University, founded in 1263 by John de Balliol. It has a curious provenance as de Balliol was compelled to found it as an act of penitence following an altercation with the Bishop of Durham, which saw him whipped in public outside the doors of Durham Cathedral. Balliol did at least get his name on the college and his crest, seen on the lower part of the Oriel (sticking out) window over the front gate. The lion is Scottish, de Balliol being the husband of Princess Devorguilla and the father of the future King Balliol of Scotland. Alumni include former Prime Ministers Herbert Asquith, Edward Heath and Harold Macmillan and politician Boris Johnson, Crown Princess Masako of Japan and two kings of Norway, Olav V and Harald V. Its most famous early master was John Wycliffe, who got into trouble with the Catholic Church for translating the Bible and suggesting that the Church was too wealthy. He was marched out of town and subsequently dug up after his death and burned by the Bishop of Lincoln, who founded Lincoln College (just round the corner in Turl St).

Now take five paces to your right and look at the Oxfam shop. Notice a small green plaque to the left of the shop which tells you that this was the first Oxfam shop, opened in 1947. Oxfam emerged from the Oxford Committee for Famine Relief, set up by the Professor of Greek, Gilbert Murray, amongst others, during the Second World War to help the Greeks, who were then starving under the Allied blockade. Look up to your right to see a blue plaque to Cecil Jackson Cole, the first Secretary of the organisation.

Now turn 90° to your left and look skywards. You will see a naked man on the top of the building across Turl Street. This is Oxford's Antony Gormley statue 'Another Time', locally dubbed 'The Angel of Broad Street' and was anonymously donated to Exeter College, atop which it stands.

Go forward to Turl Street and turn to look across Broad Street at **Trinity College**, set back from the road behind some imposing gates and fronted unusually by some 17th century cottages. Trinity was founded in 1555, by a privy counsellor of Mary Tudor called Thomas Pope who has his tomb in the chapel and his bust over the entrance to the hall. The building beside Blackwell's is known as Kettell Hall after a 17th century president of the college, who so hated long hair that he used to carry a pair of scissors to dinner in order to remove any offending locks from the students.

Keep going along Broad Street until you reach the stone heads on pillars to your right. These

Radcliffe Camera		Brasenose College		Jesus College	
	All Souls College		Lincoln College		Exeter College

are the 'Oxford Emperors'. Actually, no one knows whether they are Roman emperors, Greek philosophers or numerically challenged evangelists, but they are the third set of petrified heads placed outside the Old Ashmolean (now **The Museum of the History of Science**) and the Sheldonian Theatre since the buildings were constructed in the 17th century. The Ashmolean's original artefacts were collected by two royal gardeners, the Tradescants, who roamed around the world collecting plants and picked up a fairly random selection of 'curiosities' on the way. Elias Ashmole inherited the collection, though not without a tussle with the younger Tradescant's wife, who was mysteriously found dead in her garden pond after Ashmole moved in next door. The Ashmolean Museum was the first museum in England to be open to the public.

Along to the right, climb the steps to reach the back of the Sheldonian Theatre. This was Sir Christopher Wren's first architectural masterpiece and if you turn round and look at the back of the stone head to the left of the stairs, you will find a tiny wren in its hair. **The Sheldonian Theatre** is the University's ceremonial centre, commissioned by the 17th century Chancellor of the University and Archbishop of Canterbury Gilbert Sheldon. Walk around the right side of the building and you will find its façade, where the Archbishop's mitre and crest can be seen atop the entrance, with an appropriate Latin inscription. Matriculation and Degree Day ceremonies take place here, the latter still conducted in Latin, to the incomprehension of most of those present.

Turn round to see a beautiful 15th century building, with a large door in the centre. The door was added by Wren when he built the Sheldonian and you can see his initials at its apex and an open book beneath it with a quotation in New Testament Greek. It is through this door that students reach the Sheldonian fully robed, because the **Divinity School** building, the University of Oxford's first lecture theatre, is now used as a robing room. The interior of this building, specifically its pendant lierne vaulted ceiling displaying the crests and bosses of all its benefactors, is one of the most beautiful and impressive sights in the University and can be reached, upon payment of a small entrance fee, from the Bodleian Library. It has been used as a film location and appears in three Harry Potter movies.

Now look up to your left and you will see a **line of carvings**. These resulted from a competition between Oxford's

The Radcliffe Camera

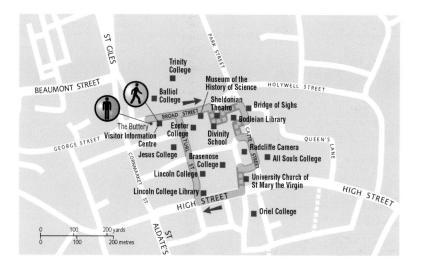

schoolchildren in 2008 and represent from left to right: the Dodo from *Alice in Wonderland*, General Pitt Rivers, the man who gave the collections to the University's Pitt Rivers Museum, Three Men in a Boat from the novel by Jerome K Jerome, Aslan the Lion from the C S Lewis *Chronicles of Narnia*, Thomas Bodley, the founder of the Bodleian Library, with a book behind his head, the Wild Boar of Boar's Head dinner fame (see walk 4), Lewis Carroll's Tweedle Dum and Tweedle Dee, Tolkien drinking beer and a Green Man.

Bear left out onto an open square with the Sheldonian behind you. Cross the square, go down the steps and ahead you will see a bridge over the roadway. Unlike its Venetian model, the Oxford **Bridge of Sighs** was built by T G Jackson in 1913 to join the two sites of Hertford College and the people sighing are thus more likely to be students going to their tutorials than prisoners.

Turn right and pause in front of a huge oak door. The door is embossed with all the crests of the colleges in existence at the start of the 17th century and is the original door of the **Bodleian Library**, the University's central library and an institution of international significance. The library was founded by Sir Thomas Bodley in 1602, a particularly propitious moment as King James I, Britain's most bookish monarch, was about to ascend the English throne. Enter the Old Schools Quadrangle and then turn to look at the tower. You can see James I in stone in the centre, giving out books to a woman on her knees. The woman represents the university and Fame stands with a verdigris trumpet to the King's right. The Tower of the Five Orders is so called because each of the columns represents a different order of classical architecture, from bottom upwards: Tuscan, Doric, Ionic, Corinthian and Composite. Around the Quadrangle you can see the original classrooms built to fill the ground floor, since books were always stored upstairs in an age without damp proofing. Above each door is the Latin name of the subject taught there.

Head through the passage, by now on your right, into

Radcliffe Square, dominated by the domed building of the **Radcliffe Camera**. Built in the mid-18th century with money bequeathed to the University by Sir John Radcliffe, Royal Physician to King William, Queen Mary and Queen Anne, this was the first round library to be built in this country, probably because it was a highly impractical shape for a library. The word Camera simply means a 'room' in Latin. Its ground floor was large, empty, and open to the elements and the library itself was reached by a spiral staircase in the centre.

Walk left around the Camera. On your left pass **All Souls College**, a leftover from the time when colleges had scholars but not students as members. This college is for researchers and many of its fellows have had to pass a fiendishly difficult examination to qualify for membership. It has a beautiful quadrangle which you can see through its gates, with its twin towers copied by Hawksmoor from Beverley Minster and a sundial presented by Wren, a former fellow of the college, on the wall to the left. This is where, in the first year of every century, a unique procession takes place before the Mallard Dinner. A huge Mallard duck flew out of the foundations when the college was founded and the procession of fellows, resplendent in their gowns, with a 'Lord Mallard' carried aloft in a Sedan Chair preceded by a fellow with a duck's head on a pole, go in search of the duck whilst singing 'The Mallard Song'.

Ahead of you is the towering gothic **University Church of St Mary the Virgin**, which served most of the University's needs before there were lecture halls or a ceremonial hall or libraries. Inside was a room containing the University Chest, a strongbox from which funds were periodically provided to poor students, and the University's first library where Oxfam held its inaugural meeting. The Oxford Martyrs (see walk 5) were tried here and you can still see the pillar broken to accommodate the stage for Archbishop Cranmer's trial.

Now look right and you will see **Brasenose College**. Named rather peculiarly after the bronze sanctuary knocker which used to grace its door, this is the college of ex-Prime Minister David Cameron, the 26th British PM to have studied at Oxford University. Walk round to the right and approach the entrance on your left; you can see a little nose poking out at the top of the door. The original knocker is in the hall, having been retrieved from a house in Lincolnshire in the 19th century whence it had been taken by students who had fled the university in the 14th century. The college had to buy the entire house in order to get it back.

Retracing your steps a short distance, continue down the alley to the right of the University Church. You have reached Oxford's High Street and opposite you will see the wall of **Oriel College**, graced by several statues of kings and bishops in all their finery. Above them all is a man dressed simply and holding a cap. This is Cecil Rhodes and the Latin legend below describes him as Caecilius Rhodos with the date of construction encoded in a chronogram. See if you can work it out.* Cecil Rhodes' legacy was the famous Rhodes Scholarships, which still exist today as post-graduate scholarships (see walks 3 and 8).

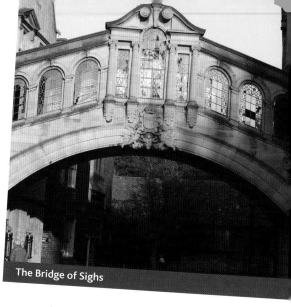

The Bridge of Sighs

Now turn right, along the High Street. Pass in front of the impressive building of the former All Saints Church, now **Lincoln College's Library.** Turn right down Turl Street to find **Lincoln College** on your right. This is the college founded in 1427 by Richard Fleming, Bishop of Lincoln, to combat Wycliffe's 'lollard heresies' and also, ironically, the college of John Wesley, father of the Methodist Church. Take a look into Lincoln's front quadrangle to find a bust of Wesley. This is a beautiful college with a set of stained glass windows by the famous Van Linge brothers in the chapel and a Lincoln Imp, symbol of the city of Lincoln, visible from the entrance over the door into the hall in the left-hand corner. This is also the college of spy writer John Le Carré and Dr Seuss, author of *Green Eggs and Ham*.

Farther along reach **Jesus College** on the left and **Exeter College** on the right. Exeter is the oldest, dating back to the 14th century and boasts a plethora of interesting alumni including: J R R Tolkien, playwright Alan Bennett, sub-4-minute mile runner Roger Bannister, writer Philip Pullman and actor Richard Burton. It was also where pre-Raphaelite artists William Morris and Burne Jones met, whose beautiful tapestry of The Adoration of the Magi can be found in the chapel along with a bronze bust of Tolkien. The front quadrangle is where Inspector Morse has his heart attack. Cross the road and look at the carvings on the front of the building. Over the Oriel window on the tower find a bespectacled woman holding her hands over her head. If you look to the right of the tower, you will find her full name written in code. Find the Marigold, next to it is an Archer, a Roundel, an Eye of God, a Lion, a Yew tree and the god Neptune. Then you will see the date, followed by more carvings: Bells, a Unicorn, Twins, a Lamb and flag, an Episcopal crozier and a Rector. See if you can work out her name.+ She was the first woman to become the head of a former men's college.

Jesus or 'the Welshmen's College' was founded by Hugh Price, treasurer of Cardiff Cathedral during the reign of Elizabeth I, who was officially named as founder. You can see the Prince of Wales feathers over the main entrance. It was the college of Lawrence of Arabia and former Prime Minister Harold Wilson whose portraits can be seen in the hall.

For refreshment, return to Broad Street and turn left to find The Buttery.

*1911

+ Marilyn Butler

St Aldate's to St Giles

WALK 2

Oxford is probably the most bookish city in England. Certainly, it has more libraries than anywhere else in the country and more published writers per square mile than anywhere else in the world. Here is a taste of literary Oxford.

Start	Finish	Distance	Refreshments
Police Station, St Aldate's	Eagle and Child, St Giles	2 miles (3.2 km)	Eagle and Child or The Morse Bar, Randolph Hotel

St Mary's Passage between Brasenose College and University Church

ON THIS WALK

Inspector Morse	Alice in Wonderland	John Betjeman
Dorothy L Sayers	Oscar Wilde	Shelley Memorial

Start outside the Police Station on St Aldate's and find the small bronze plaque on the far right of the building. Colin Dexter, the local author of the **Inspector Morse** detective series unveiled the plaque in 2006, commenting that *'There have been 89 body bags. All of the murders were solved and this is a wonderful tribute to the force.'** The television adaptations of Inspector Morse and its sequel Lewis and prequel Endeavour have been filmed all over Oxford.

Walk up St Aldate's away from the river and cross to **'Alice's Shop'.** This is the very shop where the real Alice Liddell, daughter of the Dean of Christ Church in the mid 19th century, went to buy sweets. Lewis Carroll calls it the Old Sheep Shop in *Through the Looking-Glass* because the shopkeeper looked like a sheep.

Before going to Lewis Carroll's college, take a little detour up to Brewer Street and on the left find the plaque to crime writer **Dorothy L Sayers.** The author was born here when her father was the headmaster of Christ Church Cathedral School. She studied at Somerville College and later started to write crime fiction featuring Lord Peter Wimsey. *Gaudy Night* is probably her most Oxford-centred novel with her alma mater thinly disguised as 'Shrewsbury College'.

Now return to **Christ Church Memorial Gardens,** walking through the garden and up the steps to the Broad Walk. Look right to see a noticeboard featuring Alice in Wonderland holding a pink flamingo. Lewis Carroll was a mathematician who taught at Christ Church in the 19th century and frequently went rowing with the Dean's children, entertaining them with stories featuring several people they knew, including themselves. Alice appears as herself, her sister Edith as the eaglet, Lorina as the Lori and the white rabbit was a caricature of the Dean, a nervous man whose constant refrain was *'I'm late, I'm late'.* Carroll laughed at himself too, appearing as the Dodo, because a nervous stammer made it hard for him to pronounce his real name, Charles Dodgson.

Optional: take a detour into **Christ Church** (entrance fee). The dining hall has portraits of Charles Dodgson and W H Auden and the Alice Window featuring characters from the stories. In the **Cloister** there is a plaque to Michael Llewelyn Davies who was J M Barrie's model for Peter Pan and tragically drowned aged 20.

The poplars opposite the entrance to Christ Church's Meadow Building were planted by Alice's father and if you continue a little way along the **Broad Walk,** you will find a gate to your left topped by two red hats (the symbol of Cardinal Wolsey, the college's

Evelyn Waugh		Divinity School		J R R Tolkien	
	Bodleian Library		Blackwell's		C S Lewis

founder – for both Thomas Hardy and Philip Pullman fans, this is the origin of 'Cardinal College', the name given to the college in both *Jude the Obscure and Lyra's Oxford*). Look through into the garden at the croquet lawn. Here was the inspiration for the game in *Alice in Wonderland* played with pink flamingos as mallets and hedgehogs as balls.

Continue along the Broad Walk until just before the field. From here you can see **Magdalen College's** tower, where on May Morning (1st May) at 6am the choir boys of Magdalen College School stand on the roof and sing to crowds of thousands. Magdalen was the college of Oscar Wilde, C S Lewis and John Betjeman.

Follow the path and weave your way through the gate ahead. Walk between the wall of Corpus Christi College, left, and Merton's hedge, right, until you reach another gate, and then turn right. You are now on Oxford's last cobbled street, Merton Street. Go on to face **Merton College's** entrance.

J R R Tolkien, the creator of *The Hobbit* and *The Lord of the Rings* was the Mertonian Professor of English Language and Literature. Merton was also the college of T S Eliot, author of poems including *Possum's Book of Practical Cats*, on which the *Cats* musical is based. Eliot won a scholarship to Merton, but still didn't like it much, commenting in a letter of 1914 *'Oxford is very pretty, but I don't like to be dead.'* Merton has a 'Max Beerbohm room' in honour of another of its alumni, the caricaturist and author of *Zuleika Dobson*, a quirky satire on Oxford life published in 1911, in which all the undergraduates fall in love with

a girl called Zuleika and commit mass suicide by drowning in the river.

Continue along Merton Street, which bears to the left. On your right is the **Eastgate Hotel**, which is where C S Lewis first met Joy Davidman, later his wife. At the end of the road, turn right to get a better view of **Magdalen College**, with its superb carvings. Wilde, Lewis and Betjeman studied and taught here with varying degrees of success. Oxford clearly left an impression on Wilde as he commented in *De Profundis 'The two great turning points in my life were when my father sent me to Oxford, and when society sent me to prison.'* C S Lewis was John Betjeman's tutor and he unflatteringly considered the latter an 'idle prig'. Betjeman failed his degree, but subsequently became Poet Laureate. C S Lewis created the *Chronicles of Narnia* and also wrote several books on Christianity.

Optional: take a tour of Magdalen College (entrance fee). The statues in the cloister must undoubtedly be the inspiration for some of C S Lewis's fantastical creatures. In the garden, at the end of the Addison Walk, find a plaque inscribed with his poem *What the Bird Said Early in the Year*.

Cross the road and walk left, back along the High Street, passing in front of Queen's College, until you are opposite a dome behind a wall on the other side. This is the **Shelley Memorial** and is inside University College. Occasionally open to the public, it features the recumbent dead poet, carved in white marble. Shelley had a short career at the college, expelled for writing a pamphlet entitled *On the Necessity of Atheism*. His wife, Mary Shelley, wrote *Frankenstein*.

Go past the entrance to All Souls College and turn right along Catte Street. On your left, you have the **University Church of St Mary the Virgin**. Look up to see a window on the first floor. This room contained the University's first library, the Cobham Library of 1320. Today, there are over 100 libraries in the University of Oxford. Ahead of you is the **Radcliffe Camera** which is part of the Bodleian Library and probably Oxford's best known building. Looking towards the Camera,

notice the college to the left of it. This is **Brasenose College** and alumni include John Buchan, who wrote the wartime spy story *The Thirty-nine Steps* and William Golding, who won the Nobel Prize for his novel *The Lord of the Flies*.

Continue past the quadrangle to find yourself beside another library to your right. This is the **Codrington Library** of All Souls College and has an interesting design – the exterior is plainly gothic, whilst the interior, which you can only see from outside on a dark winter's afternoon when the lights are switched on, is classical. It was designed by Nicholas Hawksmoor and is

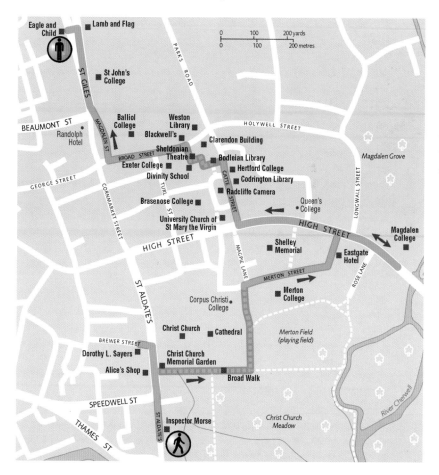

Main door of the Bodleian Library

caricatures and the initials of the man who founded it in 1602, Thomas Bodley. **Go through the oak door to find yourself in the Old Schools Quadrangle**, a beautiful square surrounded by medieval classrooms which still bear the names of the subjects studied in them in Latin over the doors. The king on the tower is Britain's most bookish, King James I, the man who commissioned the version of the Bible used in the Anglican Church. All students have the right to become readers in the Bodleian, but they still have to swear 'not to kindle any fire' in the library. Bodley's key contribution to the ongoing success of his library was a deal he struck with the Guild of Stationers, the membership organisation of all the book publishers and printers in the country, thanks to which his library was entitled to a free copy of every title published. Still today, now designated a 'copyright library', the Bodleian receives over 3,000 free books every week. The Bodleian Library has over 13 million items and in the ongoing 'Treasures' exhibition, they have displayed everything from the *Magna Carta* (of which they have four copies) to Newton's *Principia Mathematica* and Tolkien's own illustration of Smaug the dragon sitting on his hoard of gold.

guardian to the death mask of Sir Christopher Wren.

Before you leave Radcliffe Square, look at the cobbles to your left. Under these, there are two floors of book stacks built at the beginning of the 20th century to house the ever-growing collections of the Bodleian Library.

Pass out of Radcliffe Square and soon reach the front door of Hertford College to your right. This is the college of Evelyn Waugh author of *Brideshead Revisited*, Jonathan Swift, who wrote *Gulliver's Travels*, and William Tyndale, the exceptionally talented linguist who translated the Bible in the 16th century. There is a stained glass window dedicated to Tyndale in the college chapel.

Opposite, is the entrance to the **Bodleian Library**, the central library of Oxford University, the second most important library in the country and one of six British copyright libraries. Look up to see some wonderful stone

Turn right out of the square to find another courtyard opposite a large classical building. This is the **Clarendon Building** and the money to build it came from a bestseller published by the Oxford University Press (OUP) around 1703. The book was *A History of the Great Rebellion* and told the story of the English Civil War. Its author was Earl Clarendon, whose statue is clutching the book on the left-hand side of the building you are looking at. This was the OUP's first purpose-built home and produced the Bible and numerous other books until the publishing house moved to Walton Street in the 19th century (see walk 11). Prior to this, books were produced in the **Sheldonian Theatre** on your left.

Turn left and walk to the left of the Sheldonian. To your left is the beautiful 15th century building of the **Divinity School.** Above it is a medieval library called The Duke Humphry's Library. It is today the oldest reading room in the Bodleian. It also featured as the forbidden 'restricted' section of Hogwarts library where Harry looks for information about Nicholas Flamell and is almost caught by Filch, the school caretaker, when he drops his lantern.

Continue round the Sheldonian to the right onto Broad Street and you will find **Blackwell's**, the most famous bookshop in Oxford. It appeared in the *Guinness Book of Records* in the 1960s because it extended its territory under Trinity College's quadrangle to create the largest bookselling room in the world. If you want to see the Norrington Room, enter the shop through the door to the left of the pub and go downstairs. Next to Blackwells is a beautifully restored 1930s building with art deco features. Originally the 'New Bodleian', it is today the **Weston Library** and boasts two wonderful public exhibition rooms and a café. Unbelievably, it has 10 floors including a 3-storey basement.

Continue along Broad Street to Turl Street. You are now next to **Exeter College**, where Tolkien did his undergraduate studies and a bronze bust of the author can be found in the chapel. Philip Pullman is also an alumnus of Exeter and transformed it

into Jordan College in *Lyra's Oxford* and *The Northern Lights* trilogy. This is where Lyra runs across the rooftops and plays with Roger before he is kidnapped by the evil Gobblers.

Keep going until you find the Visitor Information Centre. Opposite is **Balliol College**, the alma mater of several great writers including Adam Smith, author of *The Wealth of Nations*, Graham Greene, Neville Shute, and the author of *Brave New World*, Aldous Huxley.

Farther along turn right into Magdalen Street, which will soon become St Giles; continue until you find the entrance to **St John's College.** St John's educated numerous famous poets including A E Housman, Robert Graves, Philip Larkin and John Wain as well as Jane Austen's father and brothers and Kingsley Amis. Continue up the street to find the **Lamb and Flag** pub, which appears in Thomas Hardy's, *Jude the Obscure*. Enter the pub and you will find a plaque to tell you more about it.

Finally, cross the road to the **Eagle and Child** pub. Although they occasionally repaired to the watering hole opposite, this was the main meeting place of 'The Inklings', a group of writers which included J R R Tolkien and C S Lewis. Enter the pub to find a letter signed by the members of the group, who were drinking the health of the landlord and just wanted to let him know.

Refreshment recommendation: Eagle and Child (for literary atmosphere) or the Morse Bar in the Randolph Hotel.

*as reported in The Oxford Times

Cornmarket to the Cherwell

WALK 3

This walk begins where a prison once stood at the entrance to the old town and takes you by degrees out to the freedom of the meadows by the Rivers Cherwell and Isis. Town and Gown mingle along the route, which includes the site of the tavern where Oxford's worst riot broke out in the 14th century and the launch site chosen by England's first hot air balloonist.

Start	Finish	Distance	Refreshments
Tower of St Michael, Cornmarket Street	Café Loco, St Aldate's	2¼ miles (3.4 km)	Café Loco

The Golden Cross

ON THIS WALK

Tower of St Michael | Oxford Union | Carfax Tower

Cornmarket Street | Queen Street | Covered Market

Start on Cornmarket Street at the **Tower of St Michael** at the North Gate. You are now standing at the northern entrance to the old town of Oxford beside the oldest building in the city, a defensive Saxon tower made of coral rag and built in around 1040, from the upper storey of which a doorway led out onto the city ramparts and later the Bocardo prison. Beside it, **St Michael's Church** boasts a 13th century Lily window, the oldest piece of stained glass in Oxford. If you climb up the tower, you can see the door to the cell where the Oxford Martyrs were imprisoned before they were burned on Broad Street (see walk 5). The gaol extended above your head, over the North Gate, and in the 18th century John Wesley, father of the Methodist Church, used to come here to visit prisoners.

Ahead of you is **Cornmarket Street**, so named because it was here that corn was originally sold, sheltered from the 16th century by an impressive lead roof commissioned by Corpus Christi's renowned president, John Claymond. Unfortunately, the roof was melted down during the Civil War when King Charles I made Oxford his headquarters and his soldiers needed lead shot for their muskets. Other casualties of the Civil War were the shops along Cornmarket Street, as a fire broke out in 1644 which destroyed most of them, save the beautiful specimen on the corner of Ship Street, ahead and to your left.

Turn right down St Michael's Street, passing The Three Goats Heads on your left and find the entrance to the **Oxford Union**. Cross the road for the best view. Unfortunately, you won't be able to enter unless you are a member or have made a booking to see the library, but be aware that this is the world's foremost debating society, to which heads of state, prime ministers, pop stars and the great, the good and the downright evil come to argue their case in the debating chamber, which bears an uncanny resemblance to the House of Commons. It was here that the infamous 'King and Country' debate took place in 1933, which apparently gave Hitler some unnecessary encouragement when members passed the motion 'That this House will in no circumstances fight for its King and Country'. The library has a magnificent set of recently restored Pre-Raphaelite paintings on the walls and roof depicting the legend of King Arthur.

To your right is a Grade II listed building, **Vanburgh House**, named after the architect of Blenheim Palace, who may have designed it.

At the end of St Michael's Street, note the blue plaque on the right to **Felicity Skene**, the first woman in England to be an official Prison Visitor. She kept open house for the poor and troubled here and was an early believer in the effectiveness of counselling.

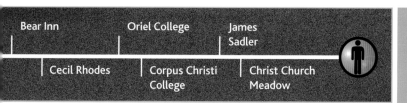

Bear Inn		Oriel College		James Sadler
	Cecil Rhodes		Corpus Christi College	Christ Church Meadow

At the T-junction, you will see the attractively Gothic **Wesley Memorial Church**, built in the 19th century just across the road from the location of the first Methodist Meeting House where John Wesley preached in the late 18th century. The church is well worth a visit. **Turn left into New Inn Hall Street** to see a plaque on the wall of the original Meeting House, in about 100 yards. Interestingly, New Inn Hall, where **St Peter's College** now stands on the opposite side of the road, was the college attended by John and Charles Wesley's grandfather. During the Civil War, it had been one of the two 'nests of Puritans' among the colleges, whose principal and students had had to flee, which meant that the hall was available for use as a makeshift mint once the King had collected all the silver plate belonging to those colleges which hadn't either hidden or buried it. Go to the Ashmolean Museum to see coins minted here, in particular the Charles I Crown.

Continue until the end of the road and at Bonn Square (see walk 7) turn left onto **Queen Street**. This used to be known as the Bailey and then Butcher's Row because in the 16th century a butchers' shambles was built here. By all accounts it was still a pretty filthy place in the 17th century, with butchers' rubbish tipped onto the street. The shambles were destroyed in the fire of 1644 along with 80 other buildings but later rebuilt.

Continue until you reach medieval **Carfax Tower**. The name Carfax comes from the Latin 'quadrifurcus' meaning crossroads and this is where the north-south and the east-west routes through the city meet, once linking the city's first four gates. It is the very centre of Oxford and was the flashpoint for a number of riots. In 1298 students attacked a bailiff here, though casualties were few, but on 10th February 1355 a town versus gown riot broke out after an argument in the Swindlestock Tavern. You can see the plaque recording this event to the left of the entrance to the Santander Bank across the road from Carfax Tower. A scholar accused the landlord of watering down his wine and threw the remainder in the man's face, at which point the landlord rushed out of the tavern, climbed Carfax Tower and rang the bell, which was the medieval town's alarm, and summoned townspeople and scholars from far and wide, all of them converging on Carfax. A fight broke out between the scholars and the townspeople, it being fairly easy to identify the former, who then wore gowns and were tonsured, and the fighting lasted for four days and nights by which time 63 students had died. Every year thereafter on the 10th February, for a period of almost 500 years (from 1356 to 1825), the Mayor had to lead a procession from the Town Hall – which is opposite you with a gold weathervane in the shape of a Ox – along the High Street to the University Church of St Mary the Virgin, to pay a silver penny for every dead student. The power of the University was clearly demonstrated in this minor but regular act of humiliation.

Beside Carfax Tower notice an old gateway with a verdigris relief of a man on horseback on top of it. This is **St Martin**, tearing his gown in two to give half to a beggar, and he is here because the tower is all that remains of St Martin's Church, which was pulled

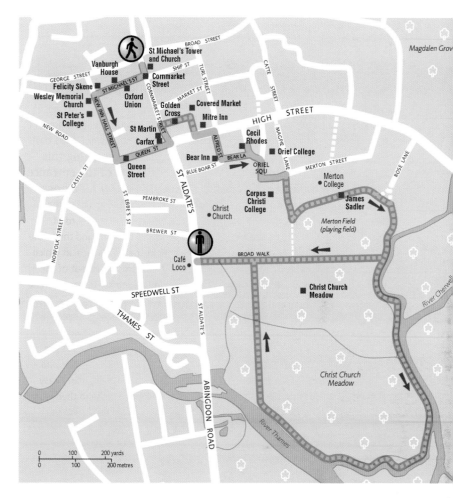

down to make way for a 19th century road-widening scheme.

Turn left back into Cornmarket Street and head over the road to enter the **Golden Cross**. There were shops here as far back as the 12th century and in the 16th century wandering players used to stay at the Golden Cross Inn, apparently including Shakespeare, whose godson was the son of the innkeeper at the Crown. If you enter Pizza Express, you can ask them to show you their 16th century wall paintings, preserved inside the restaurant.

Head into the **Covered Market** and keep straight on in order to see one of the last remaining butcher's shops. The Queen Street shambles were sold in 1773 and the butchers moved from temporary stalls in the High Street into the new Covered Market opened in 1775. Fishmongers who had previously operated from Fish Street (now St Aldate's), followed when it became illegal to sell meat and fish in the street. There is a good fishmonger here still but the real attraction of the Covered Market has to be The Cake Shop, with its sugar sculptures of everything from Oxford's Mini cars to students in subfusc – keep going and you will find it, then turn right to head back towards the High Street.

Once out of the market, cross the pedestrian crossing to the other side of the High Street. Look back to see the **Mitre Inn**, dating from about 1300, one of the oldest coaching inns in Oxford, where Catholics used to meet secretly in the crypt after the Reformation. Since the 15th century it has belonged to Lincoln College, founded by the Bishop of Lincoln, a man with a mitre. Across Turl Street beside the Inn is the former All Saints Church, now Lincoln's library.

Continue along the High Street away from Carfax and turn down Alfred Street on the right, which will take you to Blue Boar Street. At the end, on your right, find the **Bear Inn**. Now tiny, it once had thirty rooms and stabling for up to thirty horses. It is famed for its tie collection, started by the landlord in 1952. If you are wearing a tie, be prepared to have its tip severed by the bar staff.

Turn left and head down Bear Lane, briefly turning left at the end to look at the plaque to **Cecil Rhodes** on King Edward Street. Cecil Rhodes lodged here and attended Oriel College. A former Chairman of the De Beers diamond mining business and Prime Minister of Cape Colony, he is best remembered for his legacy in the form of the Rhodes Scholarships. Today these are some of the most prestigious post-graduate awards in Oxford, open to former colonies and Germany (because Rhodes approved of the Kaiser's introduction of compulsory English in schools) and now China, Malaysia and some Middle Eastern

Christ Church Meadow towards Christ Church and Merton College

countries. An unashamed imperialist, Rhodes wanted 'to promote the unity and extend the influence of the English-speaking race' and to educate world leaders who were not 'merely bookworms' and, though good scholars, also had 'qualities of manhood', exhibited 'moral force of character' and played 'manly outdoor sports'. The scholarships are now open to women as well...

Turn back into Oriel Square. To your left, **Oriel College** has a long and illustrious history reaching all the way back to the 14th century when it was founded by Adam de Brome, whose tomb you will find in its own chapel in the University Church on the High Street as he was its Rector. He was clerk to Edward II and you can see the King if you look through the entrance gate, beside Charles I, a later benefactor, underneath a particularly chubby-cheeked Virgin Mary. This is the college of the famous Elizabethan explorer Sir Walter Raleigh, Gilbert White, author of *A Natural History of Selborne* and the alma mater of most of the founders of the Oxford Movement (see walk 4). If you get a chance to enter Oriel, look out for the portrait of Cardinal Newman and Cecil Rhodes' crest in the dining hall.

At the bottom of Oriel Square follow the road round to the left into Merton Street to pass in front of **Corpus Christi College.** The college was founded in 1517 by the blind Bishop Foxe. His generous endowment did not stretch quite as far as he had anticipated but the college authorities didn't want to disappoint him, leading him twice around the quadrangle to give him the impression that it was rather larger than it actually is. Look through the entrance gate to see a column surmounted by a golden pelican. This is a perpetual calendar, enabling you to tell the time and date forever, and the pelican is the symbol of the college, because the pelican, Christ-like, plucks from its own breast to feed its young. This college was among the first to embrace the 'new learning' (which actually meant going back to some old learning and reading the Bible in the original) and had a tri-lingual Latin-Greek-Hebrew library which particularly excited the Dutch Humanist, Erasmus. It is also famous for its annual tortoise race.

Continue on Merton Street until you find a gate on your right and follow the path down the side of Merton College, passing through the kissing-gate at the end and turn left onto the path beside Merton Field. Stroll along the path, known as Deadman's Walk (see walk 10) until you come to the plaque to **James Sadler**, Oxford University lab technician and first English aeronaut, who took off from here in his balloon in 1784. If you go to St Edmund Hall, you can find his grave in the garden (originally the cemetery of St Peter in the East, which is now the College's library).

For a delightful conclusion to the route, follow the path around to the right to walk along the River Cherwell towards the Isis and enjoy the fresh air and one of the best views of the 'dreaming spires' from **Christ Church Meadow**. Return along the Broad Walk past Christ Church to St Aldate's and Café Loco or, for the energetic, complete a circuit of Christ Church Meadow.

Keble to All Souls

WALK 4

This tour takes in artistic and architectural treasures and ambles through town via the world's oldest music room along ancient alleyways to some of the earliest foundations in the University. Ideally do it in the afternoon, so you can visit *The Light of the World* at Keble College and Harris Manchester's chapel, ringing the colleges in advance to check you can enter.

Start	Finish	Distance	Refreshments
Keble College	All Souls College	1¼ miles (2 kms)	The Turf Tavern or Crypt Café

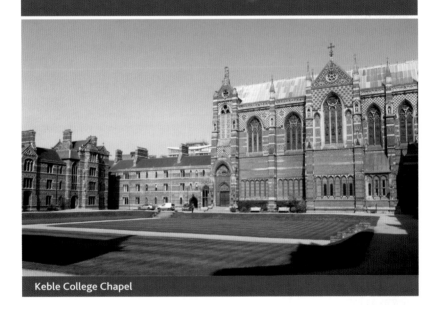

Keble College Chapel

ON THIS WALK

Keble College	Harris Manchester College	Holywell Music Room
Mansfield College	Catholic Martyrs	Turf Tavern

Start outside Keble College on Parks Road. Founded in 1870 **Keble College** is an underappreciated treasure. Greeted with derision owing to the unconventional nature of its architecture, and becoming the target of a university society, the Destroy Keble Society, membership of which was dependent on the production of a brick from the college's walls (red for term, yellow for annual and blue for life membership), and even enshrining in its statutes the freedom to move away from Oxford if conditions became unfavourable, it has nevertheless survived as a proud member of the Oxford college family.

Apart from being the first brick-built college, an innovation for which the architect, William Butterfield, made no apology, reserving his right (in the best Oxford tradition) to 'think for himself' whilst dismissing six hundred years of college architectural tradition as 'bad local stone', Keble differed from its predecessors in a number of ways. Firstly, it had no founder and thus no original endowment. John Keble was its inspiration and it was built in his name but funds were raised by public subscription from his admirers. Keble had led a movement called the Tractarian or Oxford Movement, which called for the Anglican Church to return to its 'Catholic roots'. The Movement was anti-Puritan and wanted colour, pomp and incense returned to what it saw as an increasingly drab and miserable religious experience, thus the polychromatic buildings (now somewhat dimmer than at their creation) are statements of faith. Secondly, the college was built along corridors rather than the traditional staircases, largely to make cleaning more practical. Thirdly, it was founded for 'men of modest means', taking it back to the ancient traditions of the university which trained poor boys as priests, rather than encouraging the 19th century aristocracy for whom Oxford was becoming increasingly fashionable.

Keble's chapel is breathtaking both externally and internally. The unlikely gift of a Bristol millionaire, William Gibbs, who had made his fortune importing bird droppings from South America, its height is accentuated by the sunken quadrangle beside it and its interior is a riot of colourful mosaics. *The Light of the World*, a famous Pre-Raphaelite painting by Holman Hunt depicting Christ knocking on an overgrown door to the soul, is in a side-chapel, Butterfield having refused to house it in his creation.

Continue down Parks Road past the University Museum on your left (see walk 5) and turn left down South Parks Road past Rhodes House (see walk 8). Turn right down Mansfield Road and pass **Mansfield College** on your right, which began as a training college for nonconformist ministers in

Edmond Halley	Queen's College Library		University College	
	New College	St Peter in the East Church		All Souls

The cobbles of Bath Place

2014 stone clock tower topped by a cyclist wind vane beside a gate with an elephant at its apex, both gifts from Thai benefactors. The inscription 'It's later than you think but it's never too late' comes from Dorothy L Sayers *Gaudy Night* and reflects the fact that this is a college for 'mature' students, idiosyncratically defined as 'anyone over 21'.

Continue to Holywell Street and turn left. Pass the 19th century entrance to **New College** on your right, of which more later. For now, carry on to the end of the street to find the plaque to the **Catholic Martyrs** on the wall to the right. These four men, the first two of whom were priests, were executed by Elizabeth I in 1589 and the plaque is at the site of the town gallows.

Turn back along Holywell Street and continue until you have the **Holywell Music Room** on your right. Erected in 1748, this elegant building is said to be the oldest surviving purpose-built concert hall in the world. It belongs to Wadham College (which is behind it) and has reputedly hosted Haydn. He conducted his symphony no.92, later known as the 'Oxford Symphony' in the Sheldonian in 1791.

Now turn down the cobbled Bath Place by the 17th century Bath Place Hotel, which is in a group of cottages originally built by Flemish weavers outside the city wall. Turn left through a narrow passageway, to emerge at the **Turf Tavern**, formerly known as The Spotted Cow and one of Oxford's oldest pubs. Nestling under one of the last remaining parts of the city wall, it

Birmingham and opened in Oxford in 1886 to cater for 'dissenting' students who had only just been allowed to study at Oxford University following the Reform Act of 1854. Previous to this Act and since the reign of Elizabeth I, only Anglican students had been accepted. Farther on your left pass the modern building of the **University Club**, the sports and social club of the University of Oxford.

Pass Savile Road on the right and come to the entrance of **Harris Manchester College**. Visit the chapel to see a set of windows designed by Pre-Raphaelite artists Edward Burne-Jones and William Morris with Morris' daughter May acting as model for the angels. The windows depict the six days of creation, various biblical figures and virtues and are accompanied by some fine carvings of animals and birds on the pew ends.

Harris Manchester became a full college of the University only in 1996 after a generous benefaction from Baron Harris of Peckham, the former Chairman of Harris Carpets. Look left to see a

has been the setting for many episodes of Inspector Morse and, among many noted patrons, has been frequented by former US President Bill Clinton and ex-Australian PM Bob Hawke, who holds the record for downing a yard of ale in 11 seconds, unbeaten since 1963.

Turn right through the pub to see the city wall on your left and through another narrow passage with a blue plaque to Jane Burden, William Morris's muse and wife, on the right-hand wall.

Emerge under the Bridge of Sighs (see walk 1) and turn left down New College Lane. At No. 7, find the house of **Edmond Halley**, Astronomer Royal, Professor of Geometry and identifier of Halley's Comet. Notice his observatory on the roof.

Continue along the lane between walls blackened by the burning of brown coal in the past (outlawed under the Clean Air Act of 1956) until you come to the original entrance to **New College** on your left. As you can see, this is a college which was trying to be inconspicuous, following terrible town and gown riots in Oxford in the mid 14th century and the ravages of the plague. In fact, it was founded in 1379 to train priests precisely because so many had died visiting the sick. Over the door you can see three statues. In the centre is the Virgin Mary, in whose honour the college was originally named and to either side are the Angel Gabriel and William of Wykeham, the Bishop of Winchester, founder of both New College and Winchester College public school and chief minister of King Edward III. It has a huge chapel with a Joshua Reynolds

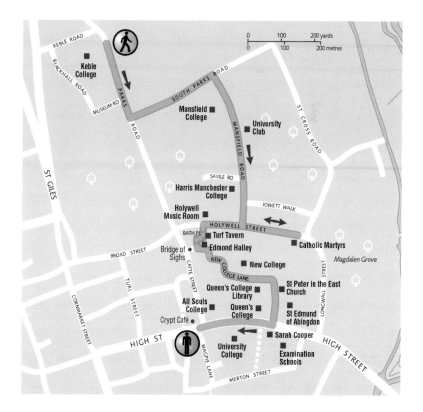

window, an Epstein statue of Lazarus rising from the dead and an El Greco painting of St James, though perhaps most charming are its medieval misericordia – wood carvings on seats at perching height for tired worshippers. See also the cloister, which features in *The Goblet of Fire,* where Harry Potter argues with Draco Malfoy and the latter is transformed into a ferret by Mad-Eye Moody. This is the college of William Spooner, responsible for original 'Spoonerisms' including a famous toast to the 'Queer old Dean' (Dear old Queen). Alumni include actors Hugh Grant and Kate Beckinsale, former Chief Rabbi Jonathan Sacks, Rick Stein and Tony Benn.

Walk under the arch and left down New College Lane.

As you round the corner, notice the red eagle crest over the door to the right and ahead of you **Queen's College's Library**, surmounted by a stone eagle, the symbol of its founder, Robert d'Eglesfield. On the left, along the wall of New College, notice the grotesques, carvings originally designed to ward off evil spirits but latterly added purely for decorative purposes. These are late 20th century by Michael Groser and feature geometric heads interspersed with all kinds of wildlife from dung beetles to a lemur.

Follow New College Lane round to the right.

On your left you pass **St Peter in the East Church**, which dates to a time before travel insurance when travellers prayed to be spared from highwaymen and disease as they left the city and praised the Lord if they made it back safely through the city gates – in this case the East Gate, which was nearby and from which the Eastgate Hotel takes its name. The church has a 12th century crypt, and the rest of the building is used as the library of St Edmund Hall. If you look up as you pass, you can see a series of carvings dating from the restoration of the church in the 1960s. The man holding the money bags was the then bursar. If you enter the college and walk around the church, you can find other carvings including one of the chaplain and his pet Labrador.

If you stop at the metal gate at the end of the wall to your left,

you can see the cemetery and a handsome bronze by sculptor Rodney Munday of the founder, **St Edmund of Abingdon**, seated and reading a book. Over the main entrance find the college crest and another chronogram giving the date of the canonisation of the founder. See if you can work out the date*. This is the college of broadcaster Sir Robin Day and if you go into the front quad, you can see an entertaining carving of him on the right-hand wall. Despite being one of the early halls of the University, 'Teddy' Hall did not become a full college until 1957.

Continue until you reach the High Street

and notice opposite you the plaque to **Sarah Cooper** of marmalade fame *(see walk 7)* before turning left to face the imposing building of the **Examination Schools** designed by T G Jackson at the end of the 19th century. This is where Oxford University students, dressed in their subfusc (black and white) uniforms, take their exams in two huge halls on the first floor, known as the North School and the South School, and there are also numerous lecture rooms used throughout the year. During the two World Wars, the building was used as a military hospital. Notice the reliefs over the entrance featuring a viva voce exam and an MA degree ceremony.

Queen's College

Cross the High Street, stopping opposite the cupola of **Queen's College**. The founder was chaplain to Queen Philippa of Hainault, the wife of Edward III. However, the Queen you see under the cupola is Queen Caroline, consort of George II and the college's patroness, who gave £2,000 towards rebuilding the college in the 18th century. Since the 15th century the college has celebrated two special annual dinners: The Needle and Thread Dinner, from a French pun on Eglesfield – aiguilles et fils; and The Boar's Head Dinner, so called after an incident involving a Queen's student in Shotover Park who was attacked by a wild boar but ably defended himself by thrusting a book by Aristotle down the boar's throat and shouting 'Graecum est!' (It's Greek!). Diners are summoned with trumpet blasts. Famous alumni include utilitarian philosopher Jeremy Bentham, Rowan Atkinson 'Mr Bean' and Sir Tim Berners Lee, inventor of the World Wide Web.

Continue along the High Street. **University College** is to your left. It is the oldest foundation in the university, dating back to 1249, and houses the Shelley Memorial (under the dome) despite having famously expelled Shelley in 1811 for publishing a pamphlet entitled 'On the Necessity of Atheism'. Famous alumni include royal physician Dr John Radcliffe, scientist Stephen Hawking and Bill Clinton.

Walk to **All Souls College** (see walk 1), founded in 1438 as both a college and a chantry, where 'All Souls of the Faithful Departed', mainly those killed during the 100 years war with France, would be prayed for. Over the entrance you can see the founder, Archbishop Chichele, on one side and Henry VI on the other, surmounted by souls rising to heaven. Former fellows of the college include architect Sir Christopher Wren, Lawrence of Arabia and philosopher Isaiah Berlin. *1246

Refreshments: Crypt Café

The Prison to the Pitt Rivers Museum

WALK 5

This walk takes in some historic and lovely buildings filled with treasures, starting with Oxford Castle and ending at the Pitt Rivers Museum. If you enter all the buildings along its length, it could take you several weeks. If not, simply enjoy exploring the area around Oxford's cultural centres and come back for a closer look another time.

Start	Finish	Distance	Refreshments
Oxford Castle	Pitt Rivers Museum	1¼ miles (2 km)	The Eagle and Child or Lamb and Flag

The University Museum of Natural History

ON THIS WALK

Oxford Castle		Old Fire Station		Burton Taylor Rooms	
	Coroner's Court		Gloucester Green		Oxford Playhouse

Start at **Oxford Castle** outside the Unlocked visitor centre. Do take a tour and see the crypt. If not, read the history of the castle on the ground outside in the stylised time-line consisting of a series of silver circles. Looking towards the visitor centre and up to the left, you can see tall **St George's Tower**, the only remaining building from the original castle of 1071 built by Robert D'Oilly, who was appointed High Sheriff of Oxfordshire by William the Conqueror shortly after the Norman Invasion. It was in this tower that Queen Matilda, daughter of Henry I (and widow of the Holy Roman Emperor), was besieged in 1142 by her cousin, Stephen, during a 19-year Civil War fought over their rival claims to the English throne. Her daring escape took place one winter's night as she descended from the tower and ran across the snow camouflaged in a white cloak. There is an 11th century crypt in St George's Tower, which you can visit if you take the tour, and which was only re-discovered when Prison Governor and amateur archaeologist Daniel Harris made his prisoners take part in excavations in the late 18th century. To the right sits the **Mound**, once the look-out post over Oxford's western entrance which conceals within it a 13th century vaulted well chamber, another of Harris's discoveries. The round building beside you is the 18th century debtors' tower, where those unable or unwilling to pay what they owed were incarcerated until the money was forthcoming.

The castle and subsequent prison have hosted several other colourful characters. Parliamentarian prisoners were held here during the Civil War by a notoriously sadistic Prison Keeper called Marshall William Smith, who was so cruel that soldiers were urged to fight to the death to avoid him. In the 17th century Anne Green survived a hanging despite her friends pulling on her legs to hasten her end (see walk 9) and in the 18th century Mary Blandy, middle-class and rather gullible, managed to murder her father by mistake. Her lover gave her a powder, supposedly a love potion designed to soften her father's opposition to their proposed marriage, which she added to her father's tea but which turned out to be arsenic. The unfortunate woman was hanged in 1752. In fact the 18th century saw 100 hangings at the prison for everything from sheep-stealing to spying and Oxford's public executioner, Jack Ketch, was so well known that he became the model for the hangman in Punch and Judy shows.

Walk towards the road alongside The Living Room, which is on the site of the 18th century gallows. The last person was executed here in 1863 and the castle was used as a prison until 1996 when it was redeveloped into the Unlocked centre, the Malmaison Hotel and the restaurants you can see today. Since then it has also done valuable service as a TV and film location, with scenes from *Inspector Morse*, *Bad Girls*, *The Bill*, *102 Dalmatians*, *The Spy Game* and *Lucky Break* all filmed here.

Ashmolean Museum

The Eagle and Child

Museum of Natural History

Martyrs' Memorial

The Lamb and Flag

Pitt Rivers Museum

At New Road look left to see **Nuffield College**, founded by car maker William Morris – note the wheels under the roof points. Turn right, passing the impressive entrance to the Malmaison Hotel, on to a building which looks like a small castle. This houses the **Coroner's Court** and underneath is a tunnel (now closed) which used to lead to the prison. On this site in the 16th century a 'foul mouthed bookseller' called Roland Jenkes, accused of plotting against Queen Elizabeth I, cursed the court and supposedly caused the deaths of at least 300 people (including two judges and several members of the jury) from a mysterious plague, the so called 'Black Assize' of 1577.

Use the crossing, after which go left and then almost immediately right down a narrow alley called Bulwarks Lane (once known as Bullocks Lane) which runs between the backs of **St Peter's** and Nuffield Colleges and still contains parts of the old city wall. If the gate on the right is open, you can look into the garden to see a section of one of the old bastions of the wall. Canal House, which you will find to your left, is now St Peter's College Master's Lodge but used to be the headquarters of the Oxford Canal Company.

Continue along this picturesque lane and at the bottom of the incline cross George Street Mews, turning right to emerge onto George Street between two restaurants. Opposite you is the Victorian gothic building of The Corn Exchange, and the **Old Fire Station**. This is now a centre for the creative arts and a social enterprise for the homeless but was Oxford's Fire Station for 100 years until 1971.

Turn right and pause opposite the lovely building of the University's **History Faculty** by architect T G Jackson, formerly Oxford's Boys School, founded by philosopher Thomas Hill Green in 1881. Alumni include comedian Ronnie Barker (hence the Four Candles 'Fork Handles' pub on your right) and *Great Egg Race* scientist Heinz Wolff. Cross over left into St Georges Place leading to **Gloucester Green**, so called because it was in the vicinity of the former Gloucester College and was once used as a bowling green. During the Civil War, Royalist troops drilled here and there were even a few hangings from a convenient nearby tree. In the 18th and 19th centuries an annual fair took place here and cattle markets were held for a time. Today there are regular markets here on Wednesdays and Saturdays (food) and Thursdays (crafts) with Farmers' markets on the first and third Thursday of every month.

Keep to the right-hand side of the square and notice the plaque just before the end of the building to your right commemorating **Privates Biggs and Piggen**, so-called 'Levellers' who rebelled against Oliver Cromwell, demanding the democracy and civil rights which had been promised them.

Continue forward, crossing Friars Entry (probably named after the Carmelite friars who lived in the vicinity) to the **Burton Taylor Rooms** on your right. Richard Burton actually studied briefly at Exeter College with Neville Coghill during his RAF training in 1944 and acted in Shakespeare's *Measure for Measure*. Promising to return, he was back in 1966 with actress Elizabeth Taylor, by now his wife, for a much-praised

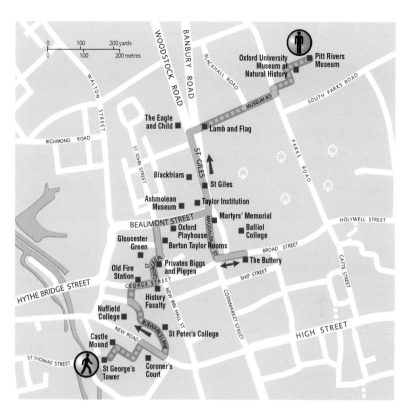

production of *Doctor Faustus*, directed by Coghill. The actors donated most of the proceeds to the Oxford Playhouse. This tiny 50-seater theatre, primarily used for student productions, was named in their honour.

Turn right into Beaumont Street to find the façade of the Oxford Playhouse. Numerous well known names from the theatre and cinema – Rowan Atkinson, Michael Palin, Dudley Moore, Richard Burton and Alan Bennett to name but a few, took their first steps towards fame and fortune on or behind the scenes of the stage of the Oxford Playhouse. Though dogged by financial difficulties for much of its history, even shutting for a few years in the 1980s, it is still providing a much needed venue and inspiration for new generations of actors and playwrights.

Opposite the theatre is the impressive building of the **Ashmolean Museum**, built by architect Charles Cockerell in the 19th century to house the ever-expanding collections of the original Ashmolean Museum in Broad Street (see walk 1) and the University Art Collection. It is impossible to do justice to this world-class university-owned museum (to which entry is free!) in a few words. However, start by looking for some treasures: the Alfred Jewel, the King Charles I crown, Powhatan's mantle, Guy Fawkes' lantern, Queen Elizabeth I's gloves, the Messiah violin; and visit the refurbished Egyptian galleries and the pre-Raphaelite masterpieces. Full days should be spent here, punctuated by leisurely lunches in its wonderfully airy rooftop restaurant.

The Malmaison Hotel, formerly Oxford Prison

The right-hand side of the building in front of you is actually the **Taylor Institution**, the home of Oxford University's Modern Languages Faculty since 1845. It houses a specialist library of over half a million books and lecture theatres and seminar rooms where the teaching of several European languages and their literatures takes place.

At the end of Beaumont Street, arrive at **St Giles.** This is the widest street in Oxford and still hosts an annual fair (now a funfair) on the first Monday and Tuesday after St Giles' Day on 1st September. Opposite you is a tall gothic memorial erected in 1841 in honour of Oxford's three protestant martyrs. Bishops Latimer and Ridley and Archbishop of Canterbury Thomas Cranmer were burnt at the stake almost 300 years previously in Broad Street by (Bloody) Mary I for their part in the English Reformation and, in particular, in helping Mary's father, Henry VIII, to divorce her mother, Catherine of Aragon. **The Martyrs' Memorial** by architect George Gilbert Scott was funded by public subscription when moves towards tolerance of Catholics were apparently becoming too much for the Oxford populace, who wanted the martyrs' horrible end at the hands of a Catholic queen remembered, the better to staunch the contemporary flow of sympathy towards Catholics engendered by the ideas of the Oxford Movement (see walk 4). Make a short detour here, turning right, past the Memorial onto Magdalen Street and left into Broad Street to the actual site of the pyre outside **The Buttery** restaurant, marked with a cross and opposite a stone plaque to the three martyrs on the wall of Balliol College. As the cross is in the middle of Broad Street, it was deemed more practical to erect the Memorial around the corner.

Retrace your steps, walk up St Giles and find the entrance to **Blackfriars** on your left. This is a permanent private hall of the University of Oxford run by Dominican friars. Established in 1994, the original

Blackfriars actually arrived in Oxford almost eight hundred years ago in 1221.

Walk on to reach **The Eagle and Child** pub with its memorable oval pub sign. There are various stories about the origin of its name, amongst them the tale of a ploy by a husband who supposedly 'found' his illegitimate child as he and his wife were passing a conveniently located eagle's nest, subsequently persuading his wife to adopt it. It was here that Tolkien, C S Lewis and other members of the Inklings literary group famously met every week to drink beer and chat about their work. Inside at the end of the bar, on the wall to the left are several mementoes of this group, including a letter signed by all of them, with their full university titles, written to advise the landlord that they had drunk to his good health. A lesser known club of which both writers were also members met diagonally across the road in **Balliol College**. The Coalbiters met to read Icelandic sagas, taking their name from the Old Norse 'Koalbiter' meaning those who snuggle up to the fire in winter, an attractive suggestion rather reminiscent of hobbit life...

Cross St Giles to the **Lamb and Flag** pub, named after the symbol of St John the Baptist, patron saint of merchant tailors (amongst others), and owned by St John's College next door, which was founded by a merchant tailor called Sir Thomas White. Enter the pub to find information about the pub's connections with everything from *Jude the Obscure* to *Inspector Morse*.

Walk under the arch and along the wall of St John's College. Presently, come to some 1970's student accommodation

opposite Victorian terraces and, at Museum Road on the left, the high walls of Keble College's modern student housing block. Eventually Museum Road reaches Parks Road. Opposite is the magnificent gothic building of the **Oxford University Museum of Natural History** with the Pitt Rivers Museum behind it.

Founded by the Regius Professor of Medicine, Henry Acland, and funded by Oxford University Press's Bible sales to the American Mid-West, the building is a treasure in itself, never mind the collections (see walk 8). Find the *Alice in Wonderland* exhibition and the live tarantulas upstairs. Obviously don't miss the dinosaurs and the huge slabs of different minerals including the petrified tree stump. If you are bringing children, make sure they touch the 'touchable specimens'.

Through the hall, don't miss the **Pitt Rivers Museum**, a unique experience and a must for Harry Potter fans, since it features the shrunken heads who talk with a Jamaican accent on the double-decker Knight Bus which Harry catches in *The Prisoner of Azkaban*. Find also the 'witch in a bottle' and the Sympathetic Magic display of all sorts of amulets to cure everything from warts to a shortage of salmon. In all there are over half a million objects here, from around the world. Collections include textiles, weapons, toys and medical instruments, boats, mummies and even a huge Canadian totem pole, the museum's largest artefact.

Refreshments: Natural History Museum Café

North Oxford

WALK

6

North Oxford's existence is inextricably linked to the appearance of women on the Oxford scene at the end of the 19th century. First, they began marrying the dons – previously forbidden for all but heads of house – and then they started to study. Many of the grand Victorian houses you see today were built to house the new academic families, and four of the original five women's colleges lie along our route.

Start	Finish	Distance	Refreshments
Somerville College	Woodstock Road/ St Margaret's Road	2½ miles (3.8 km)	The Cherwell Boathouse or Gees, Banbury Rd

Punts at the Cherwell Boathouse

ON THIS WALK

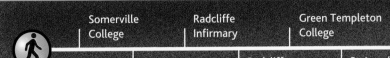

Somerville College

Radcliffe Infirmary

Green Templeton College

Language Centre

Radcliffe Observatory

St Anne's College

Begin outside **Somerville College** on the Woodstock Road. Somerville was founded in 1878, the same year as Lady Margaret Hall (LMH), after the founding committee split on the question of religion thus producing two colleges instead of one. Somerville was ecumenical while LMH was Anglican. Somerville still has an ecumenical chapel. The college is named in honour of Mary Somerville, a Scottish mathematician, scientist and advocate for women's education, and was the first women's college to employ its own tutors in 1882 and the first to acquire full college status in the University in 1951. Men weren't admitted until the early 1990s. Its best feature is undoubtedly the huge library by architect Sir Basil Champneys outside which convalescing soldiers, including the poets Siegfried Sassoon and Robert Graves, would sit under the loggia when the college served as a military hospital during the World Wars.

Alumnae include two women who were to become their respective countries' first women prime ministers – Margaret Thatcher and Indira Gandhi. Writers Vera Brittain, Iris Murdoch, Nina Bawden and Dorothy L Sayers, whose novel *Gaudy Night* was clearly based on Somerville, are also former students, as is broadcaster Esther Rantzen and politician Shirley Williams.

The history of women at Oxford is too long and tortuous to relate here, with a lot of nonsense talked by supposedly intelligent men about how academic study would induce fainting fits in the fairer sex and addle their brains, as well as pure misogynist venom, thus Dean Burgon addressing the University's women at New College in 1884 'Inferior to us God made you and inferior to the end of time you will remain!' according to Jane Robinson's eye opening book *Bluestockings*. However, despite women not being awarded degrees until 1920 and having to visit libraries with a chaperone until 1922, with numbers capped for thirty years until 1957, women now make up around 50% of the student body of the University and all colleges are now mixed.

Opposite Somerville is the entrance to the **University of Oxford's Language Centre**, where they teach at least 12 foreign languages and encourage self-study in over 140. If you look obliquely at the glass above the main entrance, you can make out the words 'Big Game Museum'. The Museum was opened here in 1906 to house a collection of stuffed animals shot by Charles Peel, an old Etonian who believed that hunting exercised 'all the faculties which go to make a man most manly' and hoped to inspire British youth to serve the Empire. The collection, including a polar bear, hippo, elephants and 'Gerald the Giraffe' moved with Peel to Exeter in 1911.

To the left of the door, you can see a blue plaque recording that the building later became the first auditorium of the Oxford Playhouse (which moved to

St Antony's College		Park Town		Sir James Murray	
	Lady Margaret Hall		Dragon School		St Hugh's College

its current home in Beaumont Street in 1938 – see walk 5), opening in 1923 with George Bernard Shaw's *Heartbreak House*.

Continue up the street away from the city centre to find the old building of the **Radcliffe Infirmary**. Opened in 1770, this was the city's main hospital for nearly 200 years. Notice the little lead money box in the wall marked 'For the support of the hospital', beyond which is the old staff entrance. It was here that great clinicians such as professors Sir Henry Acland (who pioneered the use of the stethoscope), Sir William Osler (who first encouraged medical students to talk to their patients), neurologist Sir Hugh Cairns and Sir Richard Doll, who established the link between cancer and smoking, all worked. The Radcliffe Infirmary originally catered for poor people who were sponsored by the wealthy if they were 'deserving' and its physicians and surgeons did not charge for their services. Later it enjoyed generous support from Lord Nuffield (William Morris, the car manufacturer) who founded its Nuffield Institute for Medical Research and gave £2m to establish five chairs in Surgery, Anaesthetics, Obstetrics and Gynaecology, Orthopaedics and Medicine. The first accident and emergency department in the country was opened here in one room in 1941 and in the same year the first patient was injected with penicillin by Oxford scientist Professor Florey.

Walk into the drive of the old infirmary, passing the statue of Triton (son of Poseidon, king of the sea) on your left. On your right is **St Luke's Chapel**, built by Thomas and Martha Combe, the University

Printer and his wife in 1865 (see walk 11). Make your way to the sloping building ahead of you. This is the **Mathematical Institute**. Stop to admire the Penrose Paving, an example of non-periodic tiling. Then walk through the Mathematical Institute (or around it to the right if this is not possible) to find the metal Alchemical Tree, which references a 16th century treatise on Alchemy and apparently represents 'a realisation of perfection'. From here you will also have a fabulous close-up view of the **Radcliffe Observatory**, topped by the octagonal Tower of the Winds. Built by architect James Wyatt and a functioning observatory between 1773 and 1934, when Lord Nuffield bought it. The Rotunda beside it used to house a heliometer but is now a reading room. Both of these buildings are now part of **Green Templeton College**, which was founded as a merger of the two colleges now making up its name in 2008. It is a graduate college with an emphasis on medicine, management and other social sciences relating to 'human welfare and wellbeing'. With a spirit of egalitarianism unusual for an Oxford college, it has just one common room and no High Table in the dining hall. You will find the entrance to the college a little farther along on the left with a pretty little clock tower above it.

Carry on to **St Anne's College** on the right. The round green roof of the dining hall is topped by a ship, the symbol of the college since it started its life in Ship Street. St Anne's grew out of the Society of Home Students, which was established to provide an affordable way for young women to study in Oxford. It became a full college in 1952 and opened its doors to men in 1979. Among its alumni are politician

Edwina Currie, Penelope Lively, author of Oxford children's novel *A House in Norham Gardens*, broadcaster Libby Purves, journalist Melanie Phillips and conductor, Simon Rattle. Writer Iris Murdoch was a fellow of the college.

Across Bevington Road, you come to **St Antony's College**, a graduate college founded in 1950. Its specialities are modern international history, philosophy, economics and politics and it has a Centre for Russian and Eurasian studies. Standing on part of one of the few known Roman settlements in Oxford and beside the extension of Horse and Jockey Lane, along which Charles I and his 6,000 soldiers escaped from Cromwell's troops in June 1644, St Antony's is also intimately connected with women. Its fine Gothic Revival buildings originally belonged to a pioneering Anglican sisterhood of Tractarians, the Society of the Holy and Undivided Trinity and housed the Holy Trinity Convent, the nuns running

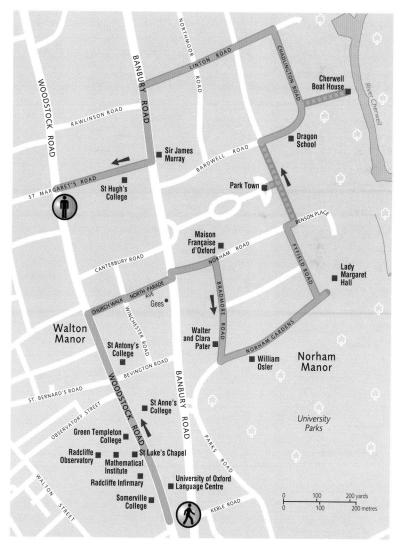

three schools and an orphanage for girls nearby. The extraordinary metal and glass **Investcorp Building** by Zaha Hadid houses a library and lecture theatre for its Middle East Centre.

Continue down the Woodstock Road and turn right down Church Walk. Cross Winchester Road and head down atmospheric North Parade Avenue, to emerge onto the Banbury Road. Turn left and cross at the pedestrian crossing, and continue down Norham Road. On your left you will come across a 1960s building with a statue of a naked woman in the garden, actually a copy of Aristide Maillol's *Flore*. This is the **Maison Française d' Oxford**, the inspiration for which goes back to the Second World War when the Free French were impressed by the fighting spirit of the English and a mutual will to work together was forged. It holds conferences, lectures, debates, French classes and has an extensive French library.

Turn right down Bradmore Road opposite to see grand houses typical of North Oxford and continue until just before the end of the road, when you can cross over to read the blue plaque on No. 2 to **Walter and Clara Pater**. Walter was a scholar and champion of the aesthetic 'Art for Art's Sake' movement, whilst his sister was an activist for women's education, who became the first classics tutor at Somerville College and privately taught writer Virginia Woolf.

At the end of the road turn left into Norham Gardens. Across the road find medical Professor **William Osler's** house at No. 13 with a square blue plaque on the wall (see walk 9). Such was his hospitality that the house was dubbed 'The Open Arms'.

Follow Norham Gardens to the end, to the red brick entrance to **Lady Margaret Hall**. Despite its rather forbidding frontage, the college has some interesting buildings by architects Sir Basil Champneys and Sir Giles Gilbert Scott, including an attractive Byzantine-style chapel, and lovely gardens bordering the River Cherwell. Founded by the Warden of Keble College, Edward Talbot, together with his wife Lavinia, who was a great promoter of women's education, the college was named after Lady Margaret Beaufort, the mother of King Henry VII and a respected patron of learning. Upon opening in 1879, its first principal was the great-niece of poet William Wordsworth, Elizabeth Wordsworth. It first accepted men in 1979. Alumni include Benazir Bhutto, first woman prime minister of Pakistan, explorer Gertude Bell, writer and historian Lady Antonia Fraser, Eglantyne Jebb, founder of Save the Children, actor Sam West and politicians Ann Widdecombe and Michael Gove.

Turn left down Fyfield Road. As you can see, most of the buildings on the right are owned by LMH.

Walk to Norham Road turning right and almost immediately left along the path with the white barrier. Half way down the path, turn left under an arch to emerge in **Park Town,** a mid-19th century development faced with Bath Stone and a very smart part of town. The small copse before you is called The Jungle and you can see a plaque on the ground to the man who planted it, explorer and early ecologist Charles Elton.

Return to the path, go left shortly to meet Bardwell Road and turn right. You are now passing between the

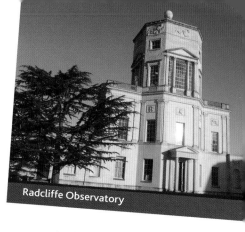
Radcliffe Observatory

buildings of the **Dragon School**, originally set up as Oxford Preparatory School in 1877 by a committee of Oxford dons who wanted a good education for their children. The leader of the committee was Mr George so it was but a short step to 'The Dragon'. The school takes both boarders and day pupils and has an impressive list of alumni including the poet Sir John Betjeman, philosopher Alain de Botton, pilot and founder of the homes for the disabled Leonard Cheshire VC, tennis star Tim Henman, geneticist J B S Haldane, actor Hugh Laurie, journalist Rageh Omar, novelist Neville Shute, jockey Sam Waley-Cohen and actress Emma Watson (Hermione to Harry Potter fans).

Notice the Dragon over the door of the last building on the right and the quirky dragon gates. Ahead of you are the school's playing fields and its war memorial.

Rounding the bend you can divert down the lane on your right, to the **Cherwell Boat House**, for an excellent lunch or to hire a punt. Otherwise keep on down Chadlington Road (continuation of Bardwell Road), then left along Linton Road and at the end turn left down the Banbury Road.

At No. 78 notice a pillar box and a blue plaque to **Sir James Murray**, lexicographer and editor of the Oxford English Dictionary. The pillar box was put here specifically for Murray's convenience because he had so much mail to post. He worked from a shed in his garden, possibly to avoid his 12 children but definitely in order to house the ever-increasing number of slips he received from contributors bearing quotations for the dictionary. The slips are reputed to have weighed 3 tonnes by the time the OED was published and came from all sorts of people including a convicted murderer in Broadmoor Hospital who alone sent him 12,000 slips.

Cross into St Margaret's Road on the right and walk to **St Hugh's College** lodge on the left. This former women's college was founded in 1886 by Elizabeth Wordsworth (see LMH) to provide affordable lodgings for women. The money came from the legacy of her father, a former Bishop of Lincoln and she named the college after Hugh of Avalon, a Bishop of Lincoln at a time when Oxford was part of the Lincoln diocese and who in fact consecrated St Giles' Church in St Giles Street in 1200. The symbol of the college is a swan because Hugh (unusually) had a guardian swan. As with Somerville, St Hugh's was used as a military hospital during the Second World War, though it specialised in head injuries. Alumnae include Aung San Suu Kyi, Burmese politician and winner of the Nobel Peace Prize, politicians Barbara Castle and Theresa May and former child maths prodigy, Ruth Lawrence.

At the end of St Margaret's Road, turn left and follow Woodstock Road back to the city centre.

Oxford's West End

WALK 7

The West End of Oxford was once a place where merchants, brewers, monks and friars lived side by side. When the Oxford Railway opened in 1844, the city's railway station was built here. More recently the area became home to Frank Cooper's Marmalade Factory. Beyond the station, Osney Island was once a village outside the city walls and home to an Augustinian friary, Osney Abbey.

Start	Finish	Distance	Refreshments
Bonn Square	Oxford Castle	2 miles (3.1 km)	Café 1071 at Oxford Castle

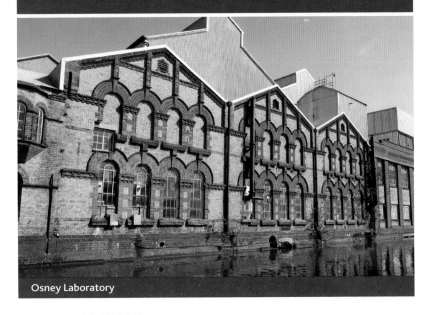

Osney Laboratory

ON THIS WALK

	Bonn Square	Roger Bacon	Lion Brewery	
	Little Gate	Quaking Bridge	St Thomas the Martyr	

Start at **Bonn Square**. For 700 years, this was a graveyard attached to the Church of St Peter-le-Bailey which stood on today's Queen Street. In 1870 burials were stopped and the church was demolished so that the street could be widened and in 1974, the square was named after Oxford's German twin town, Bonn, then the capital of West Germany. The bronze books you can now see piled up on benches and at the back of the square were a gift from Bonn to Oxford to celebrate sixty years of successful twinning from 1947-2007. They are entitled *Knowledge and Understanding* and are by sculptress Diana Bell. In the centre of the square stands the Tirah Memorial, an obelisk erected in 1900 in memory of the soldiers of the 2nd battalion Oxfordshire Light Infantry who died in 1897-8 during the Indian Tirah campaign.

Now turn round and cross Queen Street to enter St Ebbe's Street. Continue down the road, passing the unusual entrance to the **Museum of Modern Art Oxford** on your left. This museum is one of the top modern art museums in the country and well worth a visit. You will then pass Pembroke Street and **Beef Street** (unsignposted, now an entrance to Pembroke College) to the left, the former site of Beef Hall, a hall for students, generously given to the university by Nicholas Tingewick, Edward I's physician. The old southern city wall of Oxford ran along the north side of Brewer Street, which you come to next. Look up to see Pembroke's 2013 bridge linking its new buildings to its old site. On the right notice the plaque to **Sir Roger Bannister**, the man who first ran a mile in under 4 minutes in 1954. Now turn round and cross St Ebbe's to find a plaque on the wall commemorating the site of the **Little Gate**, one of the seven original gates of Oxford. There were actually two gates here, one for carts and one for pedestrians.

Continue down the road and take the first right into Turn Again Lane. See the 17th century houses at nos. 8, 9 and 10 and turn first right into Roger Bacon Lane. At the top, turn right to see the 12th century beakhead door of **St Ebbe's Church**. This stands on the site of an 11th century church dedicated to Ebbe, the daughter of the King of Northumbria. In 1224, the Franciscans built their priory outside the city wall close to this church and it stood here until 1538. The church was actually built through the city wall by special permission of King Henry III. Its site is now under the Westgate Shopping Centre.

Now turn round to walk into the Westgate Centre and take the escalator on the left to the Ground Floor. Turn immediately left at the bottom into Turn Again Lane to find a plaque to **Roger Bacon** on the left.

Osney Abbey		Osney Lock		The Jam Factory	
	Osney Island		Oxford Station		Baptists of Oxford

A 13th century Franciscan brother, Roger Bacon was also a philosopher and the closest thing to a scientist at the time, exploring maths, astronomy, optics and alchemy, predicting the invention of submarines, aircraft and cars and even suggesting that the world might be round. In his greatest book, *Opus Maius*, he champions the experimental method and the collection of evidence as the basis for a correct understanding of how the world works. He was a man ahead of his time.

Now turn back towards the shops and cross Middle Square, exiting onto Castle Street. Cross over into Paradise Street. This crossing is approximately where the West Gate into the city was once located. Continue past the imposing St George's Tower of Oxford Castle on your right (see walk 5) until you meet St Thomas' Street. To your right is

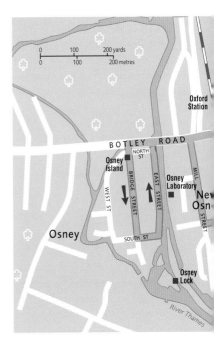

Tirah Memorial, Bonn Square

Quaking Bridge, originally wooden and first mentioned by name in 1297. Turn left to find the gate of **The Lion Brewery**, formerly Morrell's Brewery building. This was the last Oxford brewery to close after a tradition of brewing which went back to the earliest times when drinking ale was far safer than drinking water. All the medieval abbeys and the colleges had brewhouses, but almost all were destroyed in the Victorian era, leaving only Queen's College, whose brewing records go back 600 years and which only stopped in 1939. In the 19th century, professional brewers took over and from the 1920s until it closed in 1998, Morrells had a monopoly. Continue walking and, two gates further on, look to your left to see Morrells' towering industrial Victorian brewery chimney which still remains.

Continue down St Thomas' Street until you reach Hollybush

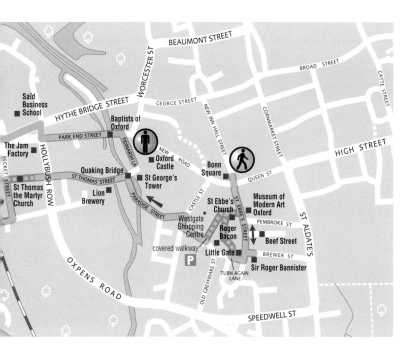

Row. Cross over and walk through the churchyard of **St Thomas the Martyr**. The church still boasts a 12th century chancel and a 13th century priest's door. It was originally a chapel built by the canons of nearby Osney Abbey and dedicated to Thomas Becket, the Archbishop murdered in Canterbury Cathedral by Henry II's knights in the 12th century.

Emerge onto Becket Street and turn left and cross the road, taking the pedestrian bridge over the railway. Go forward until you get to Mill Street. To the left is a churchyard beyond which are the last remains of **Osney Abbey** (not open to the public as they are actually in Osney Marina). Founded by Robert D'Oilly (nephew of the Robert D'Oilly who founded Oxford Castle – see walk 5) at the insistence of his wife, who apparently felt guilty about having been Henry I's mistress, the Abbey became one of the greatest Augustinian

Abbeys in England. The most notable events in its history occurred in 1222 when the first burning of a religious martyr in Europe took place here (a deacon who had converted to Judaism to marry a local Jewess) and in 1238 when the Papal Legate's brother, the chief cook, was killed. He had apparently poured boiling water over a poor scholar waiting for alms and was consequently set upon by students and shot, after which Oxford was placed under interdict. At the dissolution of the monasteries, Osney Abbey actually became Oxford's Cathedral for a couple of years with its last Abbot, Robert King, becoming the first bishop of Oxford. Henry VIII then transferred the cathedral to Christ Church. It is the Abbey's bell (Tom) which now hangs in Tom Tower at Christ Church and chimes 101 times every night at five past nine, the former college curfew. The Abbey fell into ruin, regularly plundered for building materials, only to be further destroyed by an explosion in 1643

Quaking Bridge

during the Civil War, when Charles I was storing his gunpowder in it.

Turn right and at the Botley Road go left, then turn left down Bridge Street. You are now on **Osney Island**. Today dominated by Victorian terraces, it is an increasingly fashionable place to live, with a strong sense of community. If you turn left at the end of Bridge Street into South Street, which later becomes East Street, you will find **Osney Lock** on the right, built by inmates of Oxford Prison in 1790. The prison governor, Daniel Harris, could be said to have had an unfair advantage when he tendered for the contract, since he was able to force his labourers to work for well under the market rate.

From Osney Lock, walk back along the river bank to the Botley Road. On the opposite side of the river, you will see the **Osney Laboratory** building in the old Electric Lighting Station on the site of Osney's ancient mill. The Miller of Osney appears in Chaucer's *The Miller's Tale*.

At the Botley Road, cross over and retrace your steps past a restaurant called 'The One', originally a toll house and under the railway bridge. On your left is **Oxford Station**, opened in 1844. There was a lot of controversy about the railway stopping in Oxford at all, with the Chancellor of the University, the Duke of Wellington, objecting on the grounds that it might encourage the working classes 'to move about'. The University was also worried about its undergraduates and how the railway might tempt them to go to the races at Ascot and engage in other such morally objectionable activities, so a special act of parliament was passed in 1853 allowing the University authorities to insist that railway employees stop anyone suspected of being a student and refuse to convey him for up to 24 hours even if he had paid his fare!

Continue along the road in the direction of the building with the Verdigris tower to reach **The Saïd Business School**, designed by Dixon and Jones, who also built the modern Royal Opera House in London.

Established in 1996, it is part of Oxford University and prides itself on its entrepreneurial approach to business. On the wide pavement in front of it you will find a plaque recording the location of the original railway station.

Over to your right across the road, find **The Jam Factory**. This vibrant arts centre and restaurant is on the site of Frank Cooper's original Marmalade Factory. The business began when in 1874 Frank's wife Sarah made too much marmalade for the family reasonably to consume and her husband started selling it from his grocery shop in the High Street. It became so popular that Scott took a jar on his ill-fated Antarctic expedition and, in the original Tenniel illustrations of *Alice in Wonderland*, a jar finds its way into Alice's rabbit hole.

Cross over the road and go along Park End Street. When you reach the bridge, find the sign telling you that this was where the **Baptists of Oxford** carried out their baptisms until their meeting-house was destroyed by rioters in 1715. In fact the history of the Baptists in Oxford is interesting, having begun just after the royalist garrison surrendered in 1646. According to the Victoria County History of Oxfordshire, baptisms took place 'before a scoffing crowd' and Baptists were constantly being prosecuted, even at one point dragged along to hear a sermon at the University Church of St Mary the Virgin presumably designed to encourage them to see the error of their ways. One of their leaders was a local tanner, Richard Tidmarsh, who gave his name to Tidmarsh Lane to your right. Cross the road and walk past the Registry Office and up Tidmarsh Lane to find yourself at the Castle.

Stop for refreshments at Café 1071 at the Castle.

The Saïd Business School

Scientific Oxford part 1

WALK 8

This walk takes you to the science area of the University of Oxford and to a few of the places associated with the long and distinguished history of science in Oxford, and gives you an appreciation of the truly extraordinary contribution which Oxford's scientists through the ages have made to the way we all live today.

Start	Finish	Distance	Refreshments
History of Science Museum, Broad Street	The Examinations School, High Street	1½ miles (2.5 km)	Queen's Lane Coffee House

An 'Oxford Emperor' outside the Museum of the History of Science

ON THIS WALK

Museum of the History of Science	Wadham College	Inorganic Chemistry Lab
The King's Arms	University Museum of Natural History	Rhodes House

Start outside the **Museum of the History of Science** in Broad Street. Ideally, spend an hour in this museum before you start walking. This is the original 17th century building of the Ashmolean Museum and the basement was where bodies were dissected by the Professor of Anatomy, who had the right to the corpses of prisoners hanged within 21 miles of Oxford. Some early chemical experiments also took place here. Up the steps on the raised ground floor, you will see the largest collection of astrolabes in the world and some beautiful microscopes, including a fine silver specimen which belonged to King George III. Downstairs you will find a blackboard written on in Albert Einstein's hand, dating to the time he spent lecturing in Oxford in the 1930s, camera equipment belonging to Lawrence of Arabia and to Lewis Carroll, author of *Alice in Wonderland*, and a whole case devoted to the story of the Penicillin Scientists, showing the bedpans they originally used to grow the mould and explaining how they developed antibiotics, ultimately winning the 1945 Nobel Prize for Physiology or Medicine and, more importantly, saving millions of lives.

From the steps of the museum, look left along Broad Street to see the colleges of two Nobel Prize winning scientists. **Trinity**, to the left of Blackwell's Bookshop, is the college of Sir Hans Krebs of 'Krebs cycle' fame, and Baruch Blumberg, who isolated the Hepatitis B antigen and developed a vaccine for the disease, was once the Master of **Balliol**, whose entrance tower you can see farther to the left.

Heading right, cross the street and walk to Parks Road. **The King's Arms** pub on the corner opposite you was the place where the corpses of paupers were brought in later centuries to be checked by a lawyer for foul play before they could be dissected in the basement of the Ashmolean. These were 'donated' to science in return for a Christian burial afterwards, paid for by the University.

Turn left up Parks Road and reach the entrance to **Wadham College** on your right. Wadham was founded in 1612 and later in the century it was here that the Oxford Experimental Philosophy Club met in the rooms of Warden Wilkins above the front entrance. Sir Christopher Wren, Savilian Professor of Astronomy but better known to posterity as an architect, was a member of this college and regularly attended these meetings, which eventually led to the formation of the Royal Society, the leading scientific society in this country today. Projects undertaken by the members of the Club included building clockwork flying machines, transparent beehives and the first mechanical seed drill. If you look through the entrance into the front quadrangle, you can see a clock on the left of the wall opposite which was given to his college by Wren.

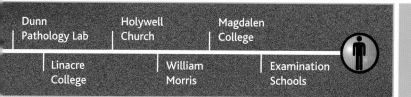

Dunn Pathology Lab	Holywell Church	Magdalen College	
Linacre College	William Morris	Examination Schools	

Continue up Parks Road, cross over South Parks Road and head for the impressive gothic building of the **University Museum of Natural History**. The science books from the Radcliffe Camera were moved here in 1861 on the initiative of Sir Henry Acland, Regius Professor of Medicine, who was largely responsible for building the Museum. He wanted the researchers here to have easy access to books. To your right is the **Radcliffe Science Library**, designed by the architect Thomas Jackson and funded by the Draper's Company of London in 1901. Beside the library is an octagonal building with four tubular chimneys. This was the first purpose-built chemistry laboratory in the University of Oxford and its design is based on the Abbot's kitchen in Glastonbury.

As you cross the grass to the entrance to the University Museum, you will notice casts of the footprints of Oxford's largest dinosaur, the Megalosaurus, parts of whose skeleton can be found inside.

Before entering, it is worth looking at the exterior of this fine building, with its carvings of plants and animals. Note that although it was built to house all the science faculties of the University, you can see carvings of Adam and Eve and an angel holding a book in one hand and a dividing cell in the other framing the front entrance. Science and religion were not yet adversaries and scientific investigation in Victorian England was based on discovering the Bible's possibilities for mankind. Indeed both Acland and the artist Ruskin, both of whom were instrumental in the founding of the museum, wanted the building to be 'a hymn to God's creation'. Both believed in Natural Theology, the theory that nature is a demonstration of divine design.

It is therefore ironic that very shortly after the Museum opened in 1860, it became the venue for the Huxley/ Wilberforce debate about evolution, when the scientist Thomas Huxley took on the Bishop of Oxford, Samuel Wilberforce. You can see a new plinth opposite the entrance commemorating this encounter. Accounts vary but most agree that the Bishop asked the scientist on which side he was related to an ape, his mother's or his father's, to which the scientist responded that he would rather be related to an ape than 'a man who used his great gifts to obscure the truth'. Upstairs inside, you can find the actual room where the debate took place, commemorated with a small gold plaque.

Now go inside. Look for the labels over the doors around the central atrium to find the departments which the museum originally housed; look at the columns, each made from a different rock of the British Isles, at the extraordinary plant carvings on each capital, each different and sculpted from live specimens from Oxford's Botanic Garden by highly skilled Irish stone masons the O'Shea brothers. Look too at the statues of scientists, in particular the latest addition, a black bust of Dorothy Hodgkin and of course, look at the breathtaking collections of geology, mineralogy, palaeontology, zoology and entomology which surround you.

You can of course spend hours in this magnificent museum, not to mention in The Pitt Rivers Museum behind it, but to continue the walk, come out of the museum, retrace your steps as far as South Parks Road and turn left. When the scientific departments of the University became too large for the University Museum, they spread naturally to the surrounding streets and in particular to South Parks Road. Shortly you will come to a small plaque on the **Inorganic Chemistry Laboratory** commemorating the achievements of Dorothy Hodgkin, who won the Nobel Prize for Chemistry in 1964 for her pioneering work in x-ray crystallography. Notoriously reported by the Daily Mail under the headline 'Oxford Housewife wins Nobel Prize' this event celebrated her achievements in determining the structure of Penicillin and of vitamin B-12. Margaret

Thatcher, the first woman prime minister of Great Britain, was among her students at Somerville College.

Pass alongside the **Dyson Perrins Laboratory**. This was endowed by the heir to the Lea & Perrins Worcestershire sauce empire and finished in 1916 by the architect Paul Waterhouse. Find the Latin inscription low down the wall behind a railing, which reads, hilariously: 'balliolensis feci hydatoecvs o si mellvs' presented as a chronogram. (If you take out the large letters and organise them according to size, starting with the largest first, you can work out the date of the building.) *

Turn to look at the circular building opposite with the green roof. This is **Rhodes House** from

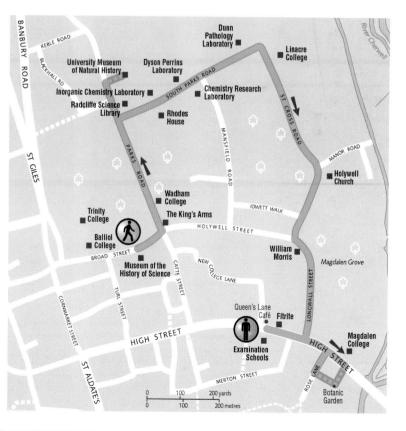

where the Rhodes Scholarships are administered. The bird on top is a copy of a Zimbabwe Bird from the ruined city of Great Zimbabwe. Zimbabwe was formerly Rhodesia. If you look across the road above the entrance, you can see a relief of the founder of Cape Town, Jan van Riebeeck's, ship Goede Hoop (Good Hope). A similar relief can be seen at the Castle in Cape Town, where Cecil Rhodes was Prime Minister in the late 19th century. Circa 95 Rhodes Scholars come to Oxford every year, benefitting from the fortune which he bequeathed to his alma mater.

Continue along the road to find various laboratories. On the right you have the new **Chemistry Research Laboratory**, a 17,000 sq.m state of the art home for researchers in the largest and probably the best chemistry department in Western Europe. It was opened by the Queen in 2004 and cost £60m.

Opposite is the Victorian red brick building of the **Dunn Pathology Laboratory**. Look for the initials WD for William Dunn on the railings at the top of the entrance steps. This is where the pioneering work on Penicillin was done in the 1930s by a team of singularly ill-assorted but brilliant scientists, Professor Howard Florey, Ernst Chain and Norman Heatley. They worked with such severely limited funds that Professor Florey forbade anyone to use the lift in the Dunn Laboratory for fear of incurring costs, and were helped by a group of poorly paid but dedicated 'Penicillin Girls'. Their main problem,

once they realised the efficacy of the mould, was growing enough of it. Their first patient, an Oxford policeman who developed septicaemia after cutting his forehead on a rose thorn, died simply because they ran out of Penicillin.

Follow the road as it turns right past **Linacre College** on your left. Note that this post-graduate college is named after Thomas Linacre, the 16th century scientist who petitioned the King to allow him to found the Royal College of Physicians, which was hugely important in ridding the country of quacks and charlatans by setting up a licensing system for medical practitioners.

Continue along St Cross Road ultimately reaching **Holywell Church**. If you are interested, take a few minutes to search for Professor Acland's grave in the Holywell Cemetery. The graveyard opened in 1847 after cholera epidemics had over-stretched the resources of the previously existing graveyards, which is interesting since Professor Acland's renown in the scientific world rests at least partially on his studies of the Oxford cholera epidemic of 1854. You might also find the grave of Kenneth Grahame, author of *The Wind in the Willows*.

Continue along Longwall Street. On your right you will see one of **William Morris's original car showrooms**. Lord Nuffield, as he later became, played a hugely important role in promoting medicine in Oxford because of the generosity of his benefactions. He endowed

*Translates as 'a Balliol man. I, Waterhouse, made this. O if only it were better!' The chronogram - **M** (1000) + **D** (500) = 1500 + **CC** (100 twice) = 1700 + **LLLL** (50 four times) = 1900 + **V V** (5 twice) = 1910 + **IIIII** (1 five times) = 1915

no fewer than five professorships – in obstetrics and gynaecology, medicine, orthopaedics, surgery and, controversially at the time, anaesthetics. He also made iron lungs in his Morris car factory, offering one to every hospital in the British Empire. He was a doctor manqué, having been unable to afford to train as a doctor in his youth but pleased to play his part when he became one of the wealthiest men in the world. He actually gave away £30 million (about £11 billion in today's money).

The Dunn Pathology Laboratory

When you reach the High Street, cross the road and turn left. Continue until you reach the entrance to the **Botanic Garden**. Go down the steps and turn right to find the plinth in honour of the Penicillin Scientists. You will find two 'Floreys' there because Professor Florey's wife also worked in the team. You are now opposite **Magdalen College**, which was, coincidentally, the site of the Hospital of St John the Baptist from 1180 for almost 300 years up to the college's foundation in 1458. The interest in science was, however, continued by the college's founder, William of Wayneflete, and has persisted throughout the college's history: the Oxford Physic Garden was founded in 1621 on land owned by the college and dedicated to growing plants for scientific and medicinal purposes (see the triumphal archway leading to Oxford Botanic Garden beside you) and the college boasts an impressive seven scientific Nobel Prize winners.[1]

Now walk towards the Botanic Garden entrance but turn right

before you get to it along the front of the Daubeny Building you will come to a door on your right with a pertinent inscription: *'Sine experientia nihil suficienter sciri potest'* (Without experimentation nothing can be sufficiently known) – the principle behind evidence-based medicine and science in general. This was written by **Roger Bacon** in his Opus Maius in the 13th century.

Now continue to Rose Lane ahead of you and turn right to return to the High Street. Cross back over, left, and walk as far as **Fitrite** shoe shop. Notice the inscription in the glass of the shop door telling you that this was where William Morris ran his cycle repair business before he diversified into cars. Look across to **The Examination Schools**, which, in both World Wars, served as a military hospital.

Now go and have some tea in the Queen's Lane Café.

[1] Magdalen's Nobel laureates are, in 'Medicine or Physiology': Charles Sherrington 1932; Howard Florey 1945; Peter Medawar 1960; Sir John Eccles 1963; In Physics Erwin Schrödinger 1933 and Anthony Leggett 2003; and in Chemistry, Robert Robinson 1947.

Scientific Oxford part 2

WALK 9

Continuing the scientific theme, this walk takes you into Christ Church, the home of the Regius Professors of Medicine and on past Corpus Christi and Merton Colleges to the High Street, where apothecaries worked and taught in 17th century Oxford. Crossing to Radcliffe Square, discover the extraordinary stories of medical science associated with the other colleges in the centre of the city.

Start	Finish	Distance	Refreshments
Christ Church	Balliol College	¾ mile (1.3 km)	The Nosebag

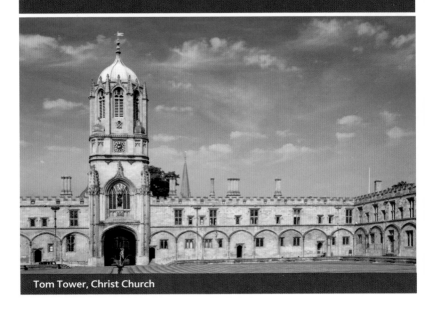

Tom Tower, Christ Church

ON THIS WALK

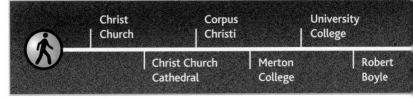

Christ Church	Corpus Christi	University College
Christ Church Cathedral	Merton College	Robert Boyle

If you have the time and resources, start at Christ Church's **Meadow Building** entrance (fee) to seek out a few monuments of scientific interest inside. Otherwise, start opposite the entrance to Merton College on Merton Street (see below).

Enter the Christ Church dining hall. On the right-hand side find the 1980s Patrick Reyntiens stained glass window with the names Willis, Acland, Osler and Garrod. This commemorates four men who contributed greatly to the development of science and medicine in Oxford and beyond.

Acland was Regius Professor of Medicine in the late 19th century and published a ground-breaking study of the Oxford Cholera epidemic of 1854 as well as founding the University Museum of Natural History (see walk 8). There is a plaque to his wife, Sarah Acland, in the Cathedral and he was physician to Alice (in Wonderland) Liddell and her family.

Osler was the Regius Professor of Medicine from 1905-1919 and despite giving his name to 'Osler's nodes' and various ailments, was keen that his tombstone should simply record that he 'brought medical students into the wards for bedside teaching'. His suggestion, revolutionary at the time, was that doctors should actually speak to their patients: 'If you listen carefully to the patient, he will tell you the diagnosis.'

By an extraordinary coincidence, Osler's car can be considered the catalyst which eventually led to William Morris (Lord Nuffield) giving some of the largest ever donations to medical science. Apparently Morris met Osler when he came to mend the latter's Renault after the radiator had cracked in freezing weather. Morris worked all night to fix it and Osler was so impressed by his dedication and expertise that he always called on him when his rather unreliable vehicle broke down. The two men became friends and when Morris became a multi-millionaire, philanthropy became his way of realising his unfulfilled medical ambitions.

Archibald Garrod was Osler's successor and discovered a whole new class of diseases determined by heredity.

Over the right-hand fireplace, find Einstein's portrait in a little yellow medallion. He was invited to Christ Church through the efforts of Lord Lindemann (see walk 10), Professor of Experimental Philosophy and later Churchill's Scientific Advisor. He received an honorary degree from the University in 1931 and accepted a Research Studentship at Christ Church with a stipend of £400 per year and a set of rooms in Tom Quad.

Opposite the Einstein window find the Alice in Wonderland window with Lewis Carroll, Alice Liddell and all the characters from the stories in blue and

| Patisserie Valerie | Brasenose College | Jesus College |
| Radcliffe Camera | Exeter College | Balliol College |

white glass. If you think this has no place in a science walk, think again. It is now widely believed that Lewis Carroll (Charles Dodgson) suffered from 'Alice in Wonderland Syndrome' a neurological disorder which manifests itself as a type of ischaemic migraine and caused him to see distorted body images, very much like the distortions in Tenniel's pictures of Alice when she gets smaller and bigger and eventually fills the whole room. It is thus probable that he was describing something that he had actually seen during an attack of migraine.

In the **Cathedral**, you can find a memorial to Robert Burton, the 17th century author of 'On the Anatomy of Melancholy' and a member of Christ Church. He was clearly himself afflicted by depression, his persona in the foreword commenting 'I write of melancholy being busy to avoid melancholy' and he eventually hanged himself in his room and was buried in the Cathedral.

Another great scientist and 'Student' of Christ Church was Sir Francis Simon, a Jewish refugee from Germany who arrived in 1933. A pioneer of low-temperature physics, he helped to make the Thermodynamics School a world-class institution.

Exit Christ Church to find yourself in Oriel Square and continue straight ahead to find **Corpus Christi** on your right. This was the college of a rather eccentric 19th century scientist, Professor William Buckland, who was Oxford University's first Reader in Geology, famous for discovering a prehistoric hyena den. It was Buckland who found the

Alice in Wonderland illustration by Sir John Tenniel

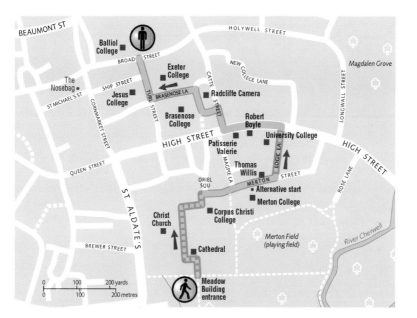

Megalosaurus whose footprints are at the University Museum and he was an expert in fossilized excrement of all types. He was also a dedicated omnivore, frequently polishing off plates of insects, moles and big game, and on one occasion eating the preserved heart of Louis XIV of France which had been kept in a silver casket at Nuneham Courtenay.

Continue along Merton Street to Merton College. Opposite Merton's entrance, find a grey plaque dedicated to **Thomas Willis**, the founder of the science of neurology. This is Beam Hall and was where he dissected heads and discovered the 'Circle of Willis', helped by Sir Christopher Wren, who illustrated his book, *Cerebri Anatome*. His insights into bi-polar disorder were surprisingly modern, though he started off as a 'pisse prophet' at local fairs, looking at people's urine and offering dubious cures for their ills.

Merton College has strong scientific credentials, being the college of John of Gaddesden, the author of Oxford's first medical textbook *Rosa Medicinae* in 1314, who was believed to be Chaucer's model for his 'Doctor of Physic' in *The Canterbury Tales*. William Harvey, the Royal Physician to King Charles I and Queen Henrietta Maria and the man who discovered that blood circulates around the body, was Warden of Merton for a year during the Civil War and hid the royal children in a bush during the Battle of Edgehill. You can see his name carved on the list of wardens in the chapel. Apparently his scientific standing was enhanced by his circulatory discoveries but it was not good for business as many of his patients considered his attacks on Galen's theories about the four humours to be dangerous nonsense.

Continue along Merton Street and turn left into Logic Lane and walk beside University College. Half way up the lane, look through the blue gate into the college on your left and crane your head round to the right to see the statue of Dr John Radcliffe in his doctor's cap, alumnus of the college and royal physician to three monarchs, who left his fortune for the foundation of a university science library. Stephen Hawking, author of *A Brief History of Time* is another University College alumnus.

Arriving at the High Street, turn left and walk along the side of University College until you reach a plaque to **Robert Boyle** who formulated Boyle's Law and Robert Hooke, his assistant and the man who first identified the living cell. This was Deep Hall in the 17th century, where these two scientists lived and worked. Along the High Street there were numerous apothecary shops at this time and the apothecaries were the first teachers of chemistry in Oxford, charging a guinea a time for demonstrations using their furnaces. Enter the **Patisserie Valerie** to read about the apothecaries who worked in this building.

Crossing over the High Street, go down Catte Street to the right of the University Church of St Mary the Virgin. In front of you find the **Radcliffe Camera**, completed in 1749 thanks to the generosity of Dr John Radcliffe's legacy at a cost of approximately £40,000, the remaining monies going to the construction of the Radcliffe Infirmary and the Radcliffe Observatory on the Woodstock Road (see walk 6). Dr Radcliffe was by all accounts a great diagnostician in an age when cures were hard to come by, owing to a basic misunderstanding of the workings of the human body. He could spot sick patients a mile off and made sure he had as little as possible to do with such cases, given the inevitability of their demise. He

made sure his patients needed nothing more than to moderate their excesses of eating and drinking – and that they were wealthy enough to pay him handsomely. Sure enough his patients generally recovered and were eager to recommend him to their acquaintances, his popularity enhanced by his naturally jovial bedside manner. In fact, many of his methods were ahead of their time: he eschewed bloodletting in favour of prescribing fresh air, exercise and moderation to his patients.

Go left around the Radcliffe Camera until you get to **Brasenose College**, which has a little bronze nose at the top of the main entrance. Here in 1650 a college fellow witnessed a miraculous recovery. Dr William Petty, together with Thomas Willis, was preparing to dissect the cadaver of a woman called Anne Green, who had been hanged for supposedly killing her illegitimate baby, when they discovered that she was still alive. The two doctors spent the whole night reviving her and massaging her back to life. She later married and had three more children.

In the 18th century another college fellow, Dr Francis Willis, famously treated King George III for his 'madness', now thought to have been porphyria. When the King apparently recovered in 1789 a medal was struck with Willis' head on it and inscribed 'Britons Rejoice Your King's restored'. Though many of his methods were crude, his belief in fresh air and exercise was, again, comparatively modern.

Continue towards the Bodleian Library and turn left down Brasenose Lane. At the end turn right into Turl Street and find the entrance to **Exeter College** on your right. This is the college where Sir Roger Bannister was a medical student when he ran the famous 'sub-four minute mile' (see walk 13), going on to become a distinguished neurosurgeon.

Opposite is **Jesus College**, identifiable by the Prince of Wales feathers over the entrance. This is the college of T E Lawrence, known as Lawrence of Arabia, who sadly required the services of a neurosurgeon after suffering head injuries in a motorcycle accident from which he later died aged 46. His portrait hangs in the hall of the college.

Continue up Turl Street until you reach Broad Street and turn left to face **Balliol College**. Lawrence was treated by Sir Hugh Cairns, the first Nuffield Professor of Surgery, who had read medicine at Balliol. Cairns was so upset by what he saw as the needless loss of life through head injuries in motorcycle accidents that he designed the first motorcycle crash helmet, thus saving thousands of lives, including those of military motorcycle despatch riders who were all issued with his helmets. His head injuries unit at St Hugh's College was dubbed 'the Nutcrackers' Suite'. Another neurosurgeon associated with Balliol

because the Master sponsored and housed him when he arrived as a refugee in 1939, was Ludwig Guttman, former Director of the Jewish Hospital in Breslau, who set up the National Spinal Injuries Centre at Stoke Mandeville hospital in Aylesbury. Believing firmly in the therapeutic nature of sport, he eventually founded the Paralympic Games.

Refreshment recommendation: Go to the Nosebag in St Michael's Street round the corner – best cakes and salads in Oxford.

Balliol College

THE MEDIEVAL JEWISH QUARTER AND THE REFUGEE SCHOLARS

The Castle to the Cemetery

WALK 10

This walk will take you through the area where the Medieval Jewish Quarter of Oxford once stood and introduce you to the history of a once vibrant community. It will then bring you up to date with the extraordinary story of the refugee scholars of the 1930s and the Hebrew collections of the Bodleian Library.

Start	Finish	Distance	Refreshments
Oxford Castle	Botanic Garden	1½ miles (2.5 km)	Grand Café

St Aldate's — once Great Jewry

ON THIS WALK

Oxford Castle	Town Hall	Moses Hall
St Ebbe's Street	New Inn Yard	Christ Church Cathedral School

Invited by William the Conqueror to follow him to England, the Jews arrived in Oxford in around 1075. They lived here until Edward I's expulsion of the entire Jewish population of England in 1290, returning only after Oliver Cromwell's readmission of the Jews in the 17th century. In the 20th century, Oxford welcomed numerous Jewish refugee scholars fleeing from the Nazis.

Start at the visitors' centre of **Oxford Castle** at the western entrance to the medieval city of Oxford. A half hour diversion at this point will take you on a tour of the Castle and the prison (which closed in 1996). In the crypt you will find an illustrated board containing information about the Medieval Jewish Quarter. This was a royal castle and a tax point and therefore important to the Jews both for business purposes and because it was somewhere they could flee to in time of trouble. It was the location of the Archa Chest (a chest with four keys, two held by Jews and two by Christians), introduced by Richard the Lionheart, where the Jews had to record all their transactions. The Constable of the Castle was duty-bound to protect 'the King's Jews', who were the direct property of the monarch and who were required to deliver one-third of their estates to the king on their death. It is also the place where Empress Matilda famously escaped across the snow when she was besieged by her cousin King Stephen during their 19-year civil war in the 12th century. The local Jews as a group were briefly imprisoned here after several incidents, sometimes simply for their protection – as were any individual Jews accused of tax arrears or more serious crimes before being transferred to the Tower of London.

Walk out of the castle precincts to New Road and turn right up the hill. Cross the road to the left and keep ahead into Queen Street. You will pass **St Ebbe's Street** on your right. In the 19th century there was a synagogue here, but tragedy struck when Rabbi Aaron Jacob and his daughter Rebecca were killed in a fire in 1844. After that, there is a record of a synagogue in Paradise Square back towards the castle. Today's synagogue is in Richmond Road in Jericho (see walk 11). It is a beautiful building and well worth a visit.

Continue along Queen Street until you get to the Carfax crossroads. Stand at the top of St Aldate's. Opposite you is the **Edinburgh Woollen Mill**. This was the house of Aaron son of Isaac, which King Stephen burned down in 1141 when the Jews refused to give him any money, declaring that they had only two weeks earlier given money to his cousin and rival, the Empress Matilda, who had arrived in Oxford ahead of him.

The next building to the right is **Oxford Town Hall** (note the golden weather

Christ Church's Refugee Scholars	Merton College	Penicillin Scientists	
Deadman's Walk	Grand Café	Bodleian Library	

vane in the shape of an Ox). In the 13th century a house on this site belonged to a wealthy Jew called David of Oxford. The rolls tell us that David wanted to divorce his wife Muriel and marry Licoricia, but was prevented from doing so by two Rabbinical Courts because his wife objected. He then appealed to King Henry III, who delightedly overruled the Beth Din and gave the divorce, something he could not have done for a Christian. After his death, David's house was of interest for another reason: The Pope had outlawed crossbows as being 'too murderously accurate', but the King wanted his army to have them, so the Jews, in the same way that they were pressed into lending money at interest, because Christians were not allowed to, were used as the King's 'get out clause' and the king housed his crossbowmen for a time in this Jewish house. The Town Hall was also where Chaim Weizmann, a Manchester chemist and the first President of the State of Israel, came to speak in 1922, having been responsible for a hugely successful conker-collecting programme during the First World War. Weizmann helped Lloyd George's war effort by using horse chestnuts as a source of acetone to make ammunition.

Continue down the right-hand side of St Aldate's until you come to **New Inn Yard**, known in the medieval period as Kepeharm's Lane, on your right. Go down this street to see the remains of a medieval building on your left, forming the ground floor of a more modern building. This was where Deulecresse (or Gedalya in Hebrew) lived in the 12th century. Pretending to limp and then be miraculously cured, Gedalya mocked Oxford's patron saint, St Frideswide, during a church

procession through the Jewish Quarter to mark her feast day. He got into such trouble with his father that he hanged himself. When his body was loaded onto a cart to be taken to London, it fell off, breaking his neck, an episode recorded as 'Frideswide's revenge' in *The Acts of the Saints*.

Return to the main street, cross over and walk to the end of the Town Hall building to see a plaque telling you that St Aldate's used to be known as 'Great Jewry'. Go round the corner to the left to find a second plaque telling you more about the Jewish Quarter.

Cross back over St Aldate's and go down Pembroke Street. With your back to the Story Museum, look across the street to see the remains of **Moses Hall**, now 'Staircase 18' of Pembroke College. Parts of the ground floor and first floor are medieval. If you cross the road and go through the tiny

passageway to the left of Pembroke College, you will see over the wall the arched windows typical of the architecture of medieval Jewish houses all over England. Moses Hall was a student residence for the University.

Walk back to St Aldate's along Pembroke Street and turn right, continuing to Brewer Street. Here, where you see the sign for **Christ Church Cathedral School**, stood the house of Vives le Long (or Chaim the tall), who was amongst 293 Jews hanged for coin-clipping in the Tower of London in 1278. King Edward I had issued his Statutum de Judesmo in 1275 which forbade the Jews from carrying on any money-lending activities and told them to go and engage in 'handicrafts and farming', for which most were singularly ill-equipped.

Look across the street – where the second tower to the left of the main entrance to Christ Church stands is the site of the medieval synagogue.

Historians think that it was probably upstairs and in a back room so as not to arouse too much unwelcome interest from the Christian Oxonians.

Cross the street and enter Christ Church Memorial Garden gate. **Christ Church** was founded in the 16th century on the land of some of the former Jewry, and a Regius Professorship of Hebrew was established for a Canon of Christ Church in 1546 though Hebrew had been studied throughout most of the University's history.

Christ Church played an important role in bringing Refugee Scholars to Oxford in the 1930s. This was largely thanks to the efforts of Lord Lindemann, a fellow of the college and Churchill's Scientific Advisor, who apparently toured Germany in his Rolls Royce, visiting Jewish scholars and inviting them to Oxford. As a key member of the Society for the Protection of Science and Learning (SPSL), he was responsible for encouraging Oxford colleges to give

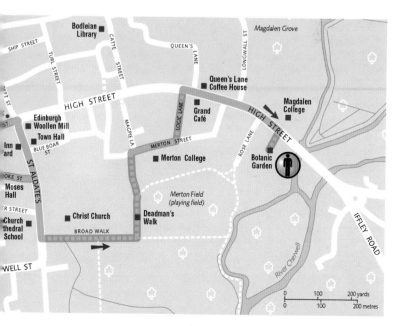

Oxford Castle's medieval tower

population brought their dead along this path outside the old city walls to their burial ground on the site of what is now the Rose Garden outside the Oxford Botanic Garden, which is just beyond the line of trees you can see across the field to your right.

Continue up the path and negotiate the kissing-gate before walking by a hedge to the right and Corpus Christi College to the left. Passing through another gate at the end, turn right into Merton Street and continue until you are facing the entrance to **Merton College**.

funds to help refugees and by the end of the Second World War, having raised £100,000, the SPSL had saved 2,500 scholars, of whom 16 went on to win Nobel Prizes, 74 to become Fellows of the Royal Society and 34, Fellows of the British Academy[1].

Probably the most famous Jewish scholar was Albert Einstein, who was invited to take up a visiting fellowship at Christ Church and stayed at the college on several occasions between the summers of 1931 and 1933. If you go into Christ Church, you can see his face in a stained glass window over the right-hand fireplace as you enter the hall.

Continue along the Broad Walk beside Christ Church's Meadow Building until you come to a path on your left. This path is known as **Deadman's Walk**. Various stories are given for the reason for this name (including the execution here of a court-martialled Civil War soldier), but it seems probable that the name goes back to the fact that the Jewish

You will see two statues above the gate. To the right is Walter de Merton, Bishop of Rochester and Chancellor of England under Edward I, who appears on the left. It was Edward I who expelled the Jews of England in 1290. Walter de Merton actually bought two houses from one of the last Oxford Jews, Jacob son of Rabbi Moses of London, in 1268 for his new college. The location of the houses is not entirely certain, but they seem to have been either in the college's Mob Quad or to the left of the gatehouse in front of you. Merton College still retains the 'starr' or contract between de Merton and Jacob in its Muniment Tower (where the college records are kept), along with four others. These contracts are written in Latin with a Hebrew addendum confirming that Jacob is speaking not only in his name but that of his wife, Hannah, and his children. Oxford is unusual in that little has changed in almost 900 years and the documents that were put in the tower in the 13th century have never moved from it. Jews did not study at the University until after the passing of

1. Source: Georgina Ferry, A Refuge for the Persecuted, Oxford Today Vol 29, No.3

The Penicillin Garden

the Reform Act of 1854, which finally allowed students of any faith to study here. Since then there have been at least 18 Jewish heads of house.

Continue along Merton Street and turn left along Logic Lane. At the High Street, turn right and walk to the **Grand Café**. This is on the site of the first coffee house opened in England and it was another 'Jacob the Jew' from the Levant, who brought coffee and possibly chocolate here for the first time in 1651. Opposite, the original **Queen's Lane Café** is thought to have been opened by another Jew called Cirques Jobson.

Continue along the High Street, crossing Merton Street until you are opposite Magdalen College and turn right towards the **Botanic Garden** entrance. On your right, you will find a monument in memory of the **Penicillin Scientists**, one of whom was a refugee scholar, Ernst Chain, who won a Nobel Prize along with Alexander Fleming and Professor Florey in 1945. Before the monument, read the inscription on the ground in grey granite which records the fact that the medieval Jewish

cemetery was on this site. Turning 90 degrees left, to the right of the imposing Danby Gate, you will find a small plaque on the wall in English and Hebrew also recording this fact. The Jews were allowed to buy the land in 1177, presumably a great relief, since prior to that they had had to take their dead all the way to London.

If you have time, visit the **Bodleian Library** by heading back up the High Street and turning right up Catte Street and past the Radcliffe Camera. The Bodleian is one of the greatest repositories of Hebrew, Yiddish and Judaeo-Arabic manuscripts and books in the world. Major collections are the Huntington Collection of 1692, which included an autographed copy of Maimonides' *Mishneh Torah*, the Oppenheimer Collection from the Chief Rabbi of Prague, which arrived here in 1829, the beautiful illuminated *Kennicott Bible*, acquired in 1771 and over 5,000 Hebrew and Arabic manuscripts from the Cairo Genizah. To find out more about these and anything else relating to Oxford's Jewish Heritage, visit www.oxfordjewishheritage.co.uk

PUBLISHERS, PRINTERS, IRONWORKERS AND BOATPEOPLE

Jericho and the Oxford Canal

WALK 11

Welcome to Jericho, once a remote part of Oxford beyond the city walls, which became an integral part of the city in the 19th century, when Lucy's Eagle Ironworks and the Oxford University Press arrived here together with their workers. Sample too the delights of the Oxford Canal, opened in 1790 to bring cheap coal to the city and today home to many attractive houseboats.

Start	Finish	Distance	Refreshments
Bus Station	Hythe Bridge Street	2¼ miles (3.5 kms)	Paddyfields on Hythe Bridge Street

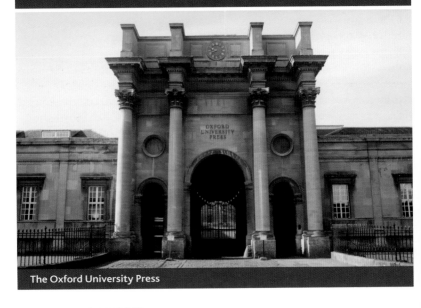

The Oxford University Press

ON THIS WALK

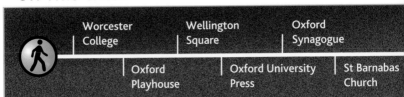

Worcester College	Wellington Square	Oxford Synagogue
Oxford Playhouse	Oxford University Press	St Barnabas Church

Start beside the bus station behind Gloucester Green in front of the '**Old School**'. Note the stone panel over the entrance featuring King Alfred (the legendary founder of the University) teaching boys on the right and St Frideswide (the Patron Saint of both Oxford and Oxford University) teaching girls on the left.

Continue left to Worcester Street, cross over and turn right. You will pass in front of **Worcester College** to the left, founded in 1714 on the site of Gloucester College after the latter had been closed during Henry VIII's dissolution of the monasteries. Continue round and cross Walton Street, to see a black panel on a concrete post on your left. This tells you that **Beaumont Palace**, which once stood on this corner, was built by Henry I and was the birthplace of both King Richard the Lionheart and his brother King John. It then became a Carmelite friary and it too was closed under Henry VIII, its stones being used to build St John's College and Christ Church.

Go up Beaumont Street, laid out in the 19th century and winning architectural historian Nikolaus Pevsner's commendation as 'the finest street ensemble in Oxford'. On the right ahead of you is the **Oxford Playhouse**. Built in 1938, it has seen many famous actors and actresses including in 1966 Elizabeth Taylor and Richard Burton, who acted in Neville Coghill's production of *Dr Faustus* and donated money to what later became the Burton Taylor rooms at the theatre.

Before you reach the theatre, turn left into St John Street, also 19th century in origin with Bath stone façades though built in cheaper brick behind. On your right is the attractive **Sackler Library**, specialising in archaeology, art history and classics.

Most of the street ahead of you belongs to the St John's College estate. It used to be said that you could walk from St John's in Oxford to St John's in Cambridge on land owned by St John's College, Oxford. Founders endowed their colleges with as much land as they could in order to provide them with an income in perpetuity since the early students certainly couldn't afford to pay fees. The estate ends where the building material changes from Bath stone to red brick just before you enter **Wellington Square**. At this point the University's Slavonic Annexe is on your left, containing a library and lecture rooms for the study of Slavonic languages and to your right is Rewley House, the University's Department for Continuing Education. High up on the wall to your right you will see a carving of a face. This is the Duke of Wellington, who was the Chancellor of the University when Wellington Square was redeveloped by Oxford University. Prior to that, this was the location of the City's workhouse, built in 1775. Earlier still,

Combe Road		St Sepulchre's Cemetery		Water fountain
	Eagle Ironworks		Elijah the Prophet		Oxford Canal

defensive earthworks passed through this area during the English Civil War, when it was known as Rats and Mice Hill. King Charles I lived in Oxford for four years during the Civil War.

Cross the square and turn left down Little Clarendon Street, a medieval street which became known as Workhouse Lane because of its location. **At the end of the street, turn right down Walton Street.** Today this is a chic part of town with a large variety of bars, restaurants and cafés.

Presently on your left you will see the imposing Corinthian portico of the **Oxford University Press (OUP)** building. Despite publishing its first books in 1478, the OUP had no purpose-built home until the beginning of the 18th century, when the Clarendon Building on Broad Street was built. In 1828, owing to the success of its business, it moved to its current, much larger site on Walton Street. The architects were Daniel Robertson and Edward Blore and the portico originally linked the south wing, which housed the Bible Press and the north wing, which housed the Learned Press. Today the OUP has numerous international offices and is the largest university press in the world, publishing over 6,000 titles per year. The OUP has its own museum here, which you can visit by appointment.

On the right you will see a fabulous building resembling a misshapen glass wedding cake. This is the eco-friendly **Blavatnik School of Government** by architects Herzog & De Meuron. Apparently it is about democracy and political transparency, hence the glass. Beside it is a building with a classical Ionic portico. Now a popular restaurant, **Freud's** building is a de-consecrated Greek Revival Church, which still sports an impressive set of stained glass windows by the 19th century artist Charles Kempe.

Cross over the road and walk down Great Clarendon Street, past the back entrance of OUP, then turn left down Wellington St. The road bears round to the right and where you see Jericho Stores on the corner, turn left into Albert Street. In front of you, you will see an unusual piece of modern architecture. With a roof designed to look like breaking waves, this is the **Oxford Synagogue**. If you look up to the right, you will see its Noah's Ark stained glass window. The Jewish community in Oxford goes back to medieval times (see walk 10) but the synagogue has been in Jericho only since the 19th century.

St Barnabas Church

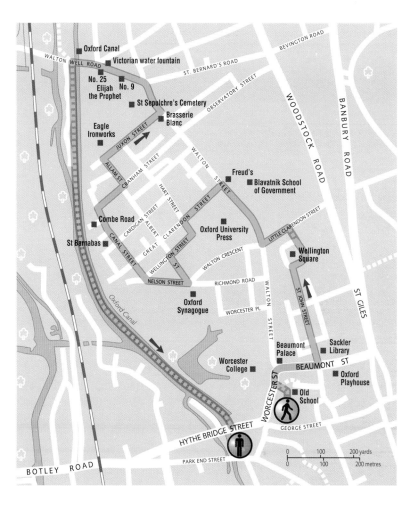

Turn right into Nelson Street and continue until you reach a small square and cross into Canal Street on the right. You will see the campanile of **St Barnabas Church** ahead to the left. Continue towards the church, but when you get to Great Clarendon Street, take a look at the very pretty three-gabled buildings of the old St Barnabas Church of England School built in 1856 now converted into houses.

At the junction with Cardigan Street, look right to see (more clearly in winter) the charming octagonal building of the Radcliffe Observatory, built with money from Dr John Radcliffe's legacy and featuring the eight winds around its summit.

To the left to see St Barnabas Church with the blue plaque on its wall. St Barnabas was founded and financed by the Superintendent of the OUP, Thomas Combe, and his wife Martha in 1869 to serve the workers of the University Press. The Combes were supporters of the Oxford Movement, rooted in the Tractarian ideas of John Keble and believed that the Anglican church should return to its Catholic origins. This is thus an Anglo-Catholic church and the architect Blomfield's basilica design is based on a church at Torcello near Venice. It warrants a mention in numerous works of literature, including Thomas Hardy's *Jude the Obscure* (where it is St Silas), Evelyn Waugh's *Brideshead Revisited* and Colin Dexter's *The Dead of Jericho*. Sir John Betjeman wrote an entire poem about it. If you can, take a look inside to see some very fine murals and an exquisitely decorated pulpit. Find also the carvings of Thomas Combe and his dog Jesse in the Lady Chapel.

Continue up Canal Street. On your left is **Combe Road** which leads to the boatyard, the focus of much recent controversy and a campaign to save it led by, amongst others, author Philip Pullman, whose 'Gyptians' in his *Northern Lights* trilogy were inspired by the people living on boats here. To the right, on the corner of Victor Street, find the Old Bookbinders pub, testament to a now rare craft.

Turn right up Cranham Street and then left down Allam Street. In front of you is a new development, but the gates bear the legend W Lucy & Co Ltd and are framed by eagles to either side. **As you turn right up Juxon Street,** look left and you will see another pair of eagles. This was the site of the **Eagle Ironworks**, belonging to W Lucy & Co, which began life as the Oxford Iron and Brass Foundry on land owned by St John's College. Its initial business in casting diversified to electrical manufacturing, which became its chief activity by the early 20th century, though agricultural machinery and street lighting remained important. In the two world wars it was a munitions factory. Philip Pullman's book *Lyra's Oxford* features a 17th century

alchemist (with a black cat daemon) whose name is Randolph Lucy and who has a laboratory on Juxon Street.

At end of Juxon Street notice Raymond Blanc's restaurant, **Brasserie Blanc** on the right. If you turn right at this point you will find more places to eat, including the Jericho Café. It is also the location of the first Phoenix Picture Houses, formerly the Oxford Kinema which screens independent, art-house and foreign-language films as well as more mainstream films and is a hugely popular cultural hub.

Turning left out of Juxon Street, continue along Walton Street and you will shortly find an iron gate on your left leading through an arch to **St Sepulchre's Cemetery**. This was opened because extra grave space was needed as the city grew larger and particularly after the cholera epidemics of 1832 and 1849. Amongst its residents are Thomas Combe and one of Balliol College's most famous masters, Benjamin Jowett, a reputedly brilliant tutor and translator of Plato.

Along Walton Street, turn left onto Walton Well Road. You will pass another entrance to the redeveloped Eagle Works. As you continue down the road and the red brick building gives way to a yellow brick tenement on your left, notice the nine carvings over the doorways. These represent scenes from the life of **Elijah the Prophet**. You can see him at No. 9 being fed by ravens having fled after he has confronted King Ahab and the priests of Baal. At No. 11 he is being fed by the widow of Zarephath, whose son is brought back from the dead at No. 13. At No. 15, Elijah stands at the entrance of the cave where he is

The Oxford Canal

hiding, then at No.17 he meets Elisha, his protégé, ploughing. At No. 19 Elijah confronts King Ahab in the vineyard which the king has stolen from Naboth after murdering him and utters the famous line 'Have you murdered and also inherited?' At No. 21 Elijah tells Ahaziah that he will never rise from his bed because he has consulted Beelzebub. In the final two carvings, Nos. 23 and 25, Elijah and Elisha cross the River Jordan on Elijah's mantle and Elijah is whisked up to heaven by a whirlwind in his fiery chariot. It is not clear why these carvings appear here, but perhaps it has something to do with the biblical Jericho.

Look right to find the **Victorian water fountain**, erected in 1885 over the well which fed this area from medieval times when cattle crossed Walton Ford to Port Meadow. Read the inscription inside it for further information.

Cross the bridge ahead of you and find a ramp on the left which descends to the **Oxford Canal**. Follow the towpath left to Hythe Bridge Street. This is particularly beautiful in spring and summer with ducks and swans and their young but is always attractive because many people live on the colourful canal boats here all year round. You will get views of the Campanile of St Barnabas and the re-developed Ironworks and passing trains. The path goes under a small footbridge and eventually leads to an iron bridge which marks the Oxford Canal terminus at Isis Lock. The Canal actually ends 200 yards farther up at Hythe Bridge Street, though there used to be a Canal Basin under the car park on the other side of the street and under Nuffield College to the left. Just before the bridge, notice the monument in the shape of a huge capstan (rope winding machine for boats). It was erected to celebrate the 200th anniversary of the Oxford Canal. For refreshment, try a dim sum lunch at Paddyfields.

Port Meadow and Wolvercote

WALK 12

This walk will take you across a thousand-year old pasture and alongside a beautiful stretch of the River Thames, frequented by boats of all kinds, to the pretty villages of Binsey and Wolvercote and a well-populated section of the Oxford Canal. In the distance, you will catch glimpses of the 'dreaming spires' of Oxford's churches and university buildings.

Start	Finish	Distance	Refreshments
Walton Well Road car park	Walton Well Road car park	6¼ miles (10 kms)	The Perch and/or The Trout

Bossom's Marina

ON THIS WALK

Port Meadow · Thames Path · Bossom's Boatyard · Binsey · Treacle Well · St Margaret's Church

Start outside Walton Well Road car park, making your way through the gate to your left and heading straight over the meadow on the path towards the river. To your right, you will see the expanse of **Port Meadow**, originally Portmaneit or Burgess Island and the place where the burgesses (or Freemen) of Oxford were allowed to graze their cattle. The area appears in the Domesday Book of 1086, when it raised 6s 8d for the king and is thought to have covered about 500 acres, including the area now occupied by the village of Wolvercote. It has never been ploughed.

During the Civil War the Royalist army was encamped in the area and drilled here. From the 17th to the 19th century, horseracing took place here and in the early 20th century part of it served as a 'flying ground' with hangars, a workshop and an airfield. It was used by the Royal Flying Corps until the outbreak of the First World War. However, none of these activities got in the way of the Freemen's rights and the cattle would always return to graze.

Continue through the small gate and over the metal bridge decked with sleepers ahead of you. On the other side of the bridge, turn right to join the **Thames Path**, the 180-mile long path which leads from the source of the Thames near Cirencester to the Thames Barrier in London.

Soon, on your left you will see canal boats and on your right a small marina for motorboats. You are now on Fiddler's Island. Ahead is the red **Medley footbridge**, erected by public subscription in 1865 with a quaintly worded plaque in the centre recording the fact. Cross over the bridge and turn right passing between **Bossom's Boatyard** on your left and a miniature dry dock on your right. It is thought that boats may have been built here for 1,000 years. Bossom's was one of the exhibitors at the first ever London Boat Show and was a family firm from 1830 until 1945. Today it prides itself on building environmentally friendly electric-powered boats.

Beyond Bossom's is the **Medley Sailing Club**, founded in 1937 and very much alive today, boasting the largest Moth sailing boat fleet in the country as well as Enterprises, Toppers and Mirrors. If you come on a Sunday afternoon or a Wednesday evening, you can watch its members racing on the River Thames here. The club is a great social hub, holding a May Morning breakfast, picnics, barbecues and punting activities on the Cherwell during the year.

Just beyond the sailing club the path forks to the left. For an hour-long diversion, head left towards historic **Binsey** village. This is where Oxford's Patron Saint, a Saxon princess named Frideswide, fled to avoid the amorous attentions of King Algar of Mercia in the 8th

Godstow Lock		Wolvercote		Trap Grounds	
	Godstow Abbey		St Edward's School		Aristotle Lane Bridge

century. She hid in the woods and in a derelict pigsty, but came out to cure the sick at the village's well, made famous as the **Treacle Well** of *Alice in Wonderland* fame. 'Treacle' in ancient times meant 'healing' but of course is taken literally by Lewis Carroll. In the story the Dormouse tells at the Mad Hatter's Tea Party, this is where three little girls, Elsie, Lacie and Tillie, live on treacle and draw things beginning with 'M' such as 'mouse-traps and the moon and memory and muchness'. The girls were of course the Liddell sisters (Lacie is Alice, Elsie is L.C. or Lorina Charlotte and Tillie was Edith's nickname). You can find the well if you head for the 12th century **St Margaret's Church**. To reach the church, turn right at the end of the track from the river and follow the road through the village and round to the right. To find the Treacle Well, look for a rectangular opening in the ground at the back of the church. This church, named after St Margaret of Antioch who famously scared off a dragon by making the sign of the cross, has yet another claim to fame. Its first vicar was England's one and only Pope, Hadrian I.

Almost the entire village is owned by Christ Church, some of whose staff (both current and retired) live in its houses. Alice Liddell, immortalised as Alice in Wonderland, was the daughter of the Dean of Christ Church and would have come walking here. Her governess, Mary Prickett, thought by some to be Lewis Carroll's model for the Red Queen, who constantly shouts 'Off with her head!' rather worryingly, lived in Church Farm, which you can find on the left as you head back towards the river.

Return towards the river via **The Perch** pub on your left. This delightful pub was apparently the first place Lewis Carroll gave a reading of *Through the Looking Glass*. For twenty years from 1928 to 1948, it was a very popular jazz venue and in 2009 was honoured at the Brecon Jazz Festival as one of the 12 venues which had made the most important contributions to jazz in the UK. It used to have a ghost, a broken-hearted soldier who had drowned himself, but since the pub burnt down in 2007, he has apparently not been spotted.

Follow the path from The Perch to the Thames Path. To your right you will now have lovely views of the river and possibly of eights and fours crews practising their rowing or sailing boats tacking back and forth. At weekends, you may also be passed by large groups of runners loudly discussing their lives and loves.

Carry on along the path. Eventually you will reach **Godstow Lock**, the last electric lock on this part of the Thames. Note the plaque on the inside wall of the lock opposite, which records its reconstruction in 1928 and opening by Lord Desborough, head of the Thames Conservancy and the man who founded the British Olympic Association.

Past the lock you come to the remains of the 12th century **Godstow Abbey**. A nunnery, founded in 1133, it was enlarged forty years later after a huge donation from Henry II, whose mistress Rosamund Clifford bore him two children and was sent to live here. Known as 'the fair Rosamund', she was buried in front of the high altar in the nunnery's church, which was where the

Bishop of Lincoln noticed her tomb and, denouncing her as a 'harlot', ordered her body to be removed. After the dissolution of the monasteries, the Abbey became Godstow House, but was severely damaged by fire during the Civil War then knocked down by General Fairfax and has been a ruin ever since.

The Liddell children, Edith, Lorina and Alice were famously enjoying a picnic at Godstow with Charles Dodgson and Robinson Duckworth, when Charles (Lewis Carroll) began to tell his *Alice in Wonderland* story.

'Alice was beginning to get very tired of sitting by her sister on the bank and of having nothing to do: once or twice she had peeped into the book her sister was reading, but it had no pictures or conversation in it,

"and what is the use of a book,"
thought Alice,
"without pictures or conversations?"'

Just past Godstow Abbey, turn off the main path up a smaller one to a road bridge on the right. There are in fact two consecutive road bridges and from the first you will get a good view of **The Trout Inn** and its charming wooden footbridge. This is where Philip Pullman's Malcolm Polstead lives in *The Book of Dust: La Belle Sauvage*, whilst baby Lyra is looked after by the nuns of Godstow Abbey. Lewis Carroll, C S Lewis and Colin Dexter's Inspectors Morse and Lewis have all enjoyed coming here.

Continue up the Godstow Road, past allotments on the left until you get to **Airmen's Bridge**. Just after the bridge you will see a memorial plaque to two airmen from the Royal Flying Corps killed in an air crash near here in 1912.

Follow the road right through the village of Wolvercote, passing the Red Lion and White Hart pubs on your left. **Wolvercote** appears in the Domesday Book as Ulfgarcote, meaning the 'Cottage of Ulfgar' and the villagers originally lived off the commons, rearing cattle and geese. In 1789 the Oxford Canal split the village into two parts and in the 19th century, the Oxford and Rugby railway was laid beside the Canal. In the 18th century, the Paper Mill (demolished in 2004) provided local employment by supplying paper to the Oxford University Press. It only ceased to make paper in 1998.

Once again beyond the houses you will come across

Port Meadow to your right. Keep right and take the little footbridge beside the road bridge to get a great view over Port Meadow. After the bridge, head down Wolvercote Green.

Go left up Church Lane and take the footpath to see **St Peter's Church** with its Palm Sunday window by acclaimed stained glass artist John Piper.

Turn right out of the churchyard down to The Plough pub and bear left on the path to a canal bridge. Cross and turn left. Continue along the towpath and under a bridge and you will see on the opposite side of the canal the playing fields belonging to **St Edward's School**, the alma mater of four RAF heroes of the Second World War: Sir Douglas Bader, Guy Gibson VC, leader of the Dambusters raids, Adrian Warburton, a leading figure in the defence of Malta and Arthur Banks who joined the Italian partisans after distinguished service in the Royal Air Force. Inside the school is a stained glass window presented by the RAF after the War in recognition of their contribution. Coincidentally, pioneering aircraft designer Sir Geoffrey de Havilland was also at school here. Other alumni include the famous actor Laurence Olivier and Kenneth Grahame, author of *The Wind in the Willows*, who may have been inspired by the nearby river.

At the far end of St Edward's grounds, you will come to a little drawbridge across the river which opens to let boats pass. Look out for the houseboats, and on a Sunday, the fishermen sitting along the bank of the canal.

There follows a series of little bridges and just to the south of

Godstow Abbey

the Frenchay Road Bridge, you will come to the **Trap Grounds reed beds** on the right. Look out for the notice board at the beginning of Frog Lane telling you all about the plants, insects, animals and birds you can expect to see here. This is one of the few places in Oxford where cuckoos breed and is a lovely addition to this walk if you have time to spare.

The next bridge you come to is the **Aristotle Lane Bridge**, which is thought to have been the route taken by King Charles I and his soldiers when he escaped from Oxford after his defeat by Oliver Cromwell's army during the Civil

War. Just before this bridge there used to be a railway station, Port Meadow Halt, which unfortunately functioned for only twenty years and closed in 1926.

When you get to Walton Well Road Bridge (which you can identify by the switch from Victorian terraces to 21st century apartments on the left-hand side), walk under the bridge and turn up the ramp on the other side to return to Walton Well Road. Cross over William Lucy Way and the railway bridge to arrive back at the car park.

The Isis and Iffley

WALK 13

This walk will acquaint you with Oxford's River Thames, known locally as the Isis, the focus of a great deal of activity in spring and summer, when rowing boats, eights boats, narrowboats and barges compete for space along its course. You will also visit the village of Iffley with its beautiful Norman church and find the track where Roger Bannister ran the first sub-4-minute mile.

Start	Finish	Distance	Refreshments
Folly Bridge	Magdalen Bridge	3¾ miles (6 kms)	Magdalen Arms, Iffley Road

Iffley Lock

ON THIS WALK

	Head of the River		Trill Mill Stream		Finish Stone	
		Salter Brothers' Boatyard		College boathouses		Desborou... Bridge

Start at the **Head of the River** pub beside Folly Bridge. This pub takes its name from the title won by the college rowing crew which finishes top of the first division in Eights Week, the University's summer rowing competition. Cross **Folly Bridge** which is one of the suggested locations for the Oxenaforda (ford for oxen) which gave Oxford its name. On your right you will see an unusually decorated house known as **'Caudwell's Castle'** after the eccentric accountant who had it built in 1849 and subsequently shot an undergraduate who was trying to deprive it of its statues. Caudwell was famously let off on the grounds that the students had been smoking cigars and drinking and were intent on 'wanton mischief'. On your left is **Salter Brothers' Boatyard**, a business which has operated for over 180 years and which was responsible for building many of the old college barges. In the First World War, Salter's produced ships for the Navy and in World War Two supplied some of the landing craft used on D-Day. Today they run pleasure boats all the way to Abingdon.

Now take the towpath to the left of the Hertford College postgraduate centre. Look left across the river to find a narrow tributary, the **Trill Mill Stream**. It runs from the Castle to St Aldates, emerging in Christ Church's Memorial Garden. Regarded as a public health risk, it was covered over in the 19th century, since when various students including T E Lawrence considered punting down it a right of passage, despite having to lie down to avoid the ceiling. An Oxford ghost story has it that one punt which entered it never came out, the skeletons of its hapless crew being found years later...

On your right sits **Grandpont House**, a three-storey Georgian house built on three arches over another tributary. Owned by Brasenose College, it has had many illustrious tenants, including the son of the Khedive of Egypt. At the end of the 19th century, it was the focus for a riot, occasioned by an attempt by Thomas Randall, a mercer and some-time mayor of Oxford who was living there, to reduce pub opening hours.

As you continue along the towpath, to your left a wonderful view opens out. Here you can see Christ Church Meadow, with Christ Church, Corpus Christi, Merton and Magdalen Colleges in the distance across the river, the ancient boundary between the Kingdoms of Wessex and Mercia.

Eventually you will see a small bridge with blue railings on the left where the **River Cherwell** joins the Thames. The Cherwell is shallow and hence the perfect place for punting, which involves pushing a flat boat along the river bed with a pole.

Beyond the Cherwell are the **college boathouses** of the University of

| Iffley Lock | | St Mary's Church | | Iffley Road Sports Complex | |
| | Grist Cottage | | Magdalen Arms | | The Plain |

Oxford. You can see college crests adorning most of them and these are usually a hive of activity in summer. To your right, you have the Queen's College recreation ground with its cricket pavilion.

If you continue along a short way, you will find the **Finish Stone** inscribed in memory of the appropriately named Colin Cox, a keen rower. This is where the Torpids and Eights rowing competitions finish. The first competition, Torpids, is in the spring term and the second and more important is Eights Week in May. Boats (each with eight rowers and a cox directing them in the stern) start 130 feet apart, a canon is fired and the aim of the exercise is to bump into the boat in front before being hit by the boat behind. Once a bump is achieved, both boats drop out and the winning boat exchanges places with the boat it hit. The crew which is in the front on the last day is usually presented with oars or 'blades' inscribed with their names.

Keep along the towpath and you come to the large black building of **University College's new boathouse**. The fact that it cost over £2m and that the previous (rather lovely) building was burnt down by arsonists in 1999 probably accounts for its fortress-like appearance.

Soon after this you will come to two small bridges, which cross the Weir Mill Stream. The **University Bathing Place** of 1868 was built here for the gentlemen of the University to bathe in privacy, but has long since fallen into disuse.

Shortly beyond the bridges on the right is a **stone pillar**, whose 1786 inscription is no longer legible, but which used to read '*Here end the liberties of Oxford*'. The path you are on is known locally as 'the gut' and is opposite 'the Kidneys', named after the shape of the area of land, now a nature reserve, on the other side of the river.

Turning the corner, you see **Donnington Bridge**, built in 1961 to ease the traffic to the East of Oxford. Continue under the bridge and the Long Bridges Nature Reserve continues to your right. This area of land was an ancient water meadow and is famous for Snake's Head Fritillary flowers and Adder's Tongue ferns and is visited in summer by reed buntings and sedge and cettis warblers.

Looking across the river you can usually see (beside the **Sea Scouts' hut**) one of the last remaining and beautifully preserved college barges. These barges afforded shelter to people watching the boat races before the college boathouses were built.

Beyond the nature reserve are a few houses. The first is **Isis Boathouse** and beyond it is Isis Cottage and then the **Isis Farmhouse**, good for a weekend lunch.

Just beyond, Iffley Lock appears to your left over a little bridge, named **Desborough Bridge** after the man who gave the Starting Ring to the University, which is the official starting point for all the bumps races. You can find this ring, which is in the shape of a bull's head with a ring in its nose if you go down the steps on the left after you cross the bridge. Lord Desborough was an outstanding athlete and keen oarsman, who twice rowed in the Boat Race against Cambridge and was Chairman of the Oxford University Boat Club. He was also the first President of the British Olympic Association and was responsible for organising the 1908 London Olympics.

As you come to the lock, you will see on your right the Mathematical Bridge, a smaller copy of Queen's College Cambridge's bridge. On your left is the lockkeeper's house with the old Thames Conservancy crest over

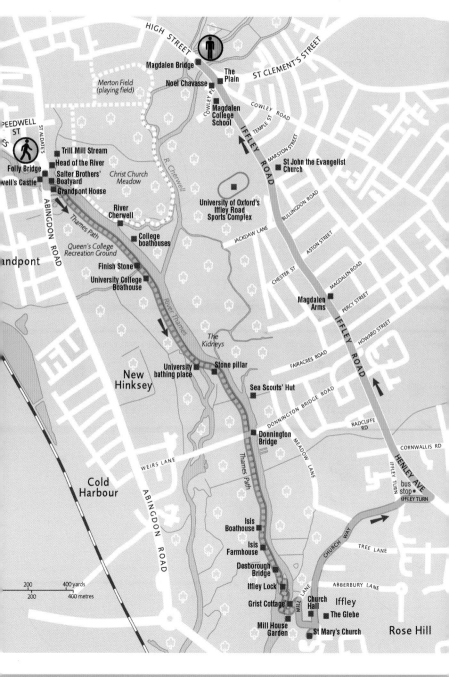

the door. The current lock is actually alongside the original pound lock, which has been converted into a weir. **Iffley Lock** was one of only three pound locks on the Thames and was originally constructed in 1623. Corpses were not allowed to cross the lock for fear of creating a right of way and coffins therefore had to be brought across by boat.

Continue along the path and cross the weir where eels used to be caught in traps. On your right as you join the road is the **Mill House Garden**. Look to the left of the gate to find a plaque telling you about the Mill. Up the road find **Grist Cottage** on your left. Notice the millstones either side of the front door. These are all that remain of the 11th century cereal mill which survived for almost 800 years until it was destroyed by fire in 1908, much to the chagrin of Lincoln College, which had owned it since 1445.

Before you is a house called Iffley Manor. The original Iffley Manor is mentioned in the Domesday Book and was later held by Walter de Merton, the founder of Merton College who used Iffley stone to build his college.

Turn right and follow the road round past the Old Parsonage and the rectory to **St Mary's Church**, enter the churchyard on your right and find the church door.

The Norman church was built in 1170 and is known as one of the best examples of Romanesque architecture in England. The entrance to the West door is beautifully preserved and its inner arch has a pattern of birds' heads and beaks found in many examples of

the architecture of this period, though no one has discovered what they represent. The outer part of the arch incorporates signs of the zodiac and of the four evangelists. If you walk round the church to your right, you will see a similarly decorated arch around a window on the tower. In the 13th century an anchoress named Annora lived in a cell beside the church. Most of her family had been put to death by King John and this was probably the safest place she could find.

If the church is open, go inside to see a beautiful example of the work of John Piper. The Nativity stained glass window was given to the church by the artist's wife in his memory in 1996. The birds and the lamb are grouped around the Tree of Life and are speaking Latin, which miracle, according to medieval legend, occurred when Christ was born. Opposite is Roger Wagner's 2012 'Flowering Tree' window.

In the churchyard, look at the Yew tree. Some writers have claimed that the Iffley Yew dates back to Saxon times and certainly the size of its trunk bears this out.

Leaving the churchyard, walk along the road opposite the entrance. On your right is **The Glebe**, land originally given to the vicar from which to support himself. On your left is the **Church Hall**. Originally a farm building and later a wheelwright's shop, this became a school in 1838 but closed down in 1961. You can still see the inscription 'Parochial School 1838' over the central door and 'Infant School 1854' over the right-hand door.

Continue down Church Way, past Tree Lane, the former

'Sheepway' which was an old drovers' route, eventually leaving the village of Iffley. Cross over the roundabout and continue until you reach Henley Avenue. Here turn left either to pick up a bus taking you down to the end of the Iffley Road or continue walking until you reach the **Magdalen Arms** across the road on your right, which is the perfect place for lunch or a drink. It used to be quite a rough pub but has been completely re-vamped and is now enjoying rave reviews as the best foodie pub in East Oxford.

Whether making your way on foot or by bus, you will eventually find a long wooden fence. If you are on a double-decker, you will be able to see over it into the **University of Oxford's Iffley Road Sports Complex** with its running track. Across Iffley Road is **St John the Evangelist Church** which played a key role in encouraging Roger Bannister to attempt his record when he ran the first sub-4-minute mile (in fact 3mins 59.4 seconds) in front of 3,000 spectators in May 1954. On the day of the race the weather was damp and windy and it was only after 6pm when the flag on the top of the church dropped, signalling that the wind had calmed, that the Olympic athlete decided to go ahead with his record-breaking attempt. The man who kept time for the race was Harold Abrahams, 100-metre Olympic champion in 1924 and hero of *Chariots of Fire*. Twenty-five year old Bannister was a medical student at Exeter College at the time, later becoming a consultant neurologist and Master of Pembroke College. Continuing to the entrance to the stadium, you will find a plaque commemorating the event.

Door of St Mary's Church, Iffley

Head along Iffley Road towards Magdalen Bridge. Notice on your left **Magdalen College School**, now one of the highest achieving schools in the country, and crossing Cowley Place find on the left a blue plaque to one of their former students, **Noel Chavasse**, another medic, who won the Victoria Cross in the First World War for repeatedly returning to rescue wounded men whilst under fire.

On your right is **The Plain** roundabout. See if you can find the Peace Stone under one of the lampposts. This was erected to celebrate the Treaty of Paris in 1814.

The restored Victorian Water Fountain to your right in the middle of the road at the entrance to **Magdalen Bridge** stands on the site of the former Toll House. It was constructed with money donated by the Morrell brewing family to celebrate the Diamond Jubilee of Queen Victoria.

If you now feel like relaxing on the river, you can find punts for hire on the River Cherwell on the right-hand side of Magdalen Bridge.

Headington to University Parks

WALK
14

This walk starts in attractive Old Headington, a settlement which appears in the Domesday Book as 'Hedintone' and dates back to Saxon times, when it was the site of a palace of the Kings of Mercia and possibly the birthplace of Oxford's patron saint, St Frideswide. It then takes you along an ancient path down to the River Cherwell and the beautiful University Parks.

Start	Finish	Distance	Refreshments
London Road, Headington	Keble Gate, University Parks	4 miles (6.3 kms)	King's Arms, Broad Street

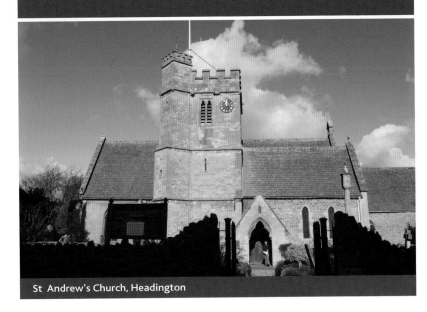

St Andrew's Church, Headington

ON THIS WALK

Cuckoo Lane	Ethelred Court	John Radcliffe Hospital
St Andrew's Church	Osler Road	Bill Heine's shark

Take a number 8, 9 or U1 bus from the High Street and get off at the Headington Shops stop on London Road. You will come up the steep Headington Hill, a Royalist stronghold in the Civil War until General Fairfax took it for the Parliamentarians, and along the London Road, previously a turnpike road created in 1775 when this became the main route from Oxford to London.

When you get off the bus, retrace your steps to the crossroads, known as Headington Carfax. Across the road to the left is **Windmill Road**, where a windmill stood from at least the 13th century. In 1788 there was a tragic accident when the miller let a young boy up to look at the mill and the boy was pulled into it and killed.

Turn right onto Old High Street (there is a car park here on the right behind Waitrose if you have come by car). Continue down the left-hand side of the road to find a tiny entrance to Cuckoo Lane on your left. Originally an important route, **Cuckoo Lane** was reduced at this point to its current narrowness in 1804. The lane used to start in Barton but it now starts here and continues down to the bottom of Headington Hill. The arch you can see about 20 yards down the lane was created to carry the drive of Headington House to the lodge which originally existed on London Road.

Continue up the Old High Street to find Headington House on your left, the entrance framed by pineapple-topped pillars. Notice the blue plaque to **Isaiah Berlin**, the first President of Wolfson College and a renowned philosopher, who lived here from the 1950s. The house was actually built for William Jackson, University Printer and founder in 1753 of *Jackson's Oxford Journal*, the precursor to today's local Oxford newspaper, *The Oxford Times*.

After Headington House, turn left up the Croft and walk between handsome high walls, past the modern architecture of Headington Baptist Church on the right and find a clutch of **17th century cottages** at the second turning on the left. Take a very brief detour to find, at the end on the right, the mounting block from which people used to climb onto their horses at the back of the White Hart pub.

Emerge onto St Andrew's Road opposite No. 3 which has a blue plaque to **Salvador de Madariaga**, a politician and philosopher who became a refugee from the Spanish Civil War and was made the first King Alfonso XIII Professor of Spanish at Oxford University. Another famous Spaniard who stayed here (at No. 1) in the summer of 1941 was the poet Luis Cernuda, who wrote poems about both the churchyard and about Cuckoo Lane.

Turn left and find yourself very soon outside the **White Hart** pub, which

The Britannia		Headington Hill Hall		Parson's Pleasure	
	boundary stone		Mesopotamia Walk		University Parks

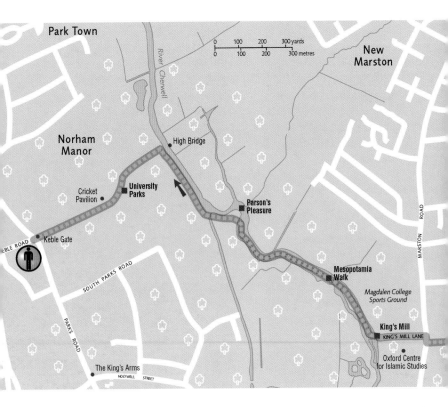

dates from the late 17th century and was once kept by the notorious Joan of Headington, who is reputed to have offered students and academics 'other services' along with their ale.

On your right is **St Andrew's Church**, with its delightful column sundial in the churchyard. This is Headington's oldest surviving building and, if you have time, go inside to see its 12th century chancel arch, 13th century south aisle and arcade and the Simon de Montfort window. In the graveyard, see if you can find to the left of the path and surmounted with two stone skulls the memorial to John Young, who died in 1688 at the age of 100. It has recently been renovated so that you can read its witty inscription 'Here lyeth John, who to the King did belong, he liv'd to be old and yet dyed Young.' As you leave the churchyard, notice the attractive Church House opposite, its doorway framed by ionic pillars and pretty wooden shutters on its windows.

At end of St Andrews Road you can make a small detour bearing right into Dunstan Road to find **Ethelred Court** on the left, the site of Ethelred the Unready's 10th century palace, but otherwise, before St Andrews Road turns into Dunstan Road, turn left along **Osler Road**, named after the famous Regius Professor of Medicine whose greatest legacy was that he made his students actually visit patients. As he rightly said, 'He who studies medicine without books sails an uncharted sea, but he who studies medicine without patients does not go to sea at all.' Another of his famous pronouncements was that men should retire at 67, spend a contemplative year off and

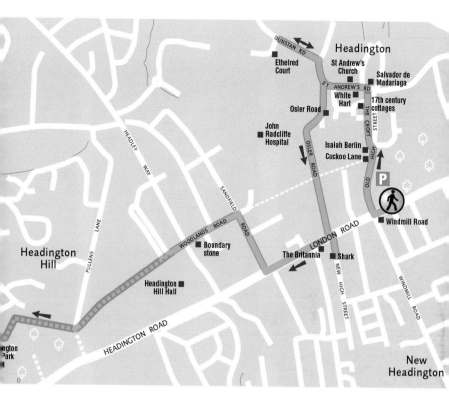

then be 'peacefully extinguished' with chloroform.

Appropriately, Osler Road runs along the back of the **John Radcliffe Hospital** (which you can see over the wall). The hospital was named after the royal physician to three British monarchs (William and Mary and Anne) because the land of Headington Manor House was bought in 1919 by the treasurer of the Radcliffe Infirmary which his legacy had paid for. It first opened as a tuberculosis hospital. Perhaps this location was chosen because of the quality of the air, which in Headington is said to resemble Champagne in contrast to the 'flat beer' of Oxford air. Today the JR is one of the four hospitals of the Oxford University Hospitals NHS Trust.

Note the continuation of Cuckoo Lane to the right of the private Manor Hospital, though our route takes us on a minor detour to see Oxford radio presenter Bill Heine's famous **shark**, so continue on past the bowling green and cross over London Road to New High Street. You really can't miss the fibreglass shark whose rear end soars above No. 2. Apparently Heine put it there in 1986 to express his feelings of 'impotence, anger and desperation' about Chernobyl, Nagasaki and nuclear power...(?!) It weighs four hundredweight and is 25 foot long but, despite Oxford City Council's refusing it retrospective planning permission, Heine was allowed to keep it there after an appeal to the Secretary of State for the Environment on the grounds that 'an incongruous object can become accepted as a landmark after a time.'

Return to London Road and turn left, passing the Britannia pub on your left. **The Britannia** was one of the original coaching inns along the route to London built in the 1770s and used to own over 8 acres of land where coach horses could graze and be stabled. You can still see the old stable building on the right.

Continue down London Road and at the pedestrian crossing cross over and then turn right up Sandfield Road. Passing the entrance to the Manor Hospital on your right, turn left up Woodlands Road. This is a continuation of Cuckoo Lane and at the end to the right of the path you will find a **boundary stone**, almost illegible, which once read '1892 F.W. AXTELL MAYOR W. S. CARTER SHERIFF' and marked the boundary between Headington and Oxford. You can just make out the ripples of the water under a now obscured Ox, the symbol of Oxford City which once graced the top of the stone. The Axtells founded the stone masons, now Symm & Co, the family firm responsible for some of the finest stonework in Oxford.

Cross Headley Way into the continuation of Woodlands Road, but don't bear right with the road (which will become Franklin Road) instead continuing straight ahead into the next part of Cuckoo Lane, this time marked with wooden posts and a memorial stone bearing a picture of a cuckoo. Walk behind the playing fields of Headington School and along past Oxford Brookes University's halls of residence. When you come to a gate on

your left, you can make a detour to see **Headington Hill Hall**. Undoubtedly the grandest building in Headington, it was built for the Morrell brewing family and was the former 'council house' of the infamous publisher Sir Robert Maxwell, but now serves as Oxford Brookes University's administrative centre. If they let you in, look for the impressive Samson stained glass window by Nechemia Azaz designed to exemplify Maxwell's personal qualities. This is in fact the second version of the window, the first having smashed whilst being loaded onto the lorry transporting it to Headington, leaving Maxwell with a glassless window for six months, an inconvenience he apparently endured with unusual sangfroid.

Continue down the extension of Cuckoo Lane passing allotments to your right and enter **Headington Hill Park** via a gate on the left for a pretty walk down to Marston Ferry Road. Leave the park by the right-hand exit at the foot of the hill to find yourself opposite the new stone building of the Oxford Centre for Islamic Studies, with its domed mosque and minaret, designed to fuse the best of Islamic and Oxonian architectural traditions.

Cross the road and head down the track, right of the Islamic Centre framed by two small obelisks and signposted 'Footpath to University Parks'. On your right is Magdalen College sports ground. At the end of the track, go through the gate and across the bridge over the weir. **King's Mill** is on your right, a mill site recorded in the Domesday Book and which had a working mill until the early 19th century. You are now walking down **Mesopotamia Walk**, so called because it is a path between two branches of the River Cherwell, a lovely peaceful walk with plenty of geese, swans, ducks and other waterfowl to observe along the way. See if you can find the bench with the inscription which begins ORE STABIT FORTIS ... and work out what it means. Contrary to appearances, it is not actually in Latin.*

Continue down the path, ignoring a bridge off to the right, but crossing the hump-backed bridge over the weir until you get to a point where you have to go over a bridge to your left which takes you to a kissing-gate. Come out of the gate and cross over the path so that you are on a little patch of ground with a large weir to your right. This is **Parson's Pleasure**, where the dons of the University of Oxford used to bathe naked until 1991. A well-known anecdote involves the Warden of Wadham, Maurice Bowra; when once a female undergraduate came past in a punt and caused all the assembled men to leap to cover their private parts, he alone covered his head with a towel, remarking 'Well, gentlemen, I don't know about you, but in Oxford I am known by my face'.

Return to the path farther along on the left and then pass through another kissing-gate to enter the University Parks proper. You are now at Cox's Corner, formerly the Parks' rubbish tip, hence its height above the river. Continue along the riverside walk until you get to the High Bridge built in 1924 and from the top of which you get a beautiful view up and down the river.

The **University Parks** belonged to Merton College until the University bought them in the mid 19th century. Claims that they were used in the Civil War for drilling practice are apparently unsubstantiated, but Charles II supposedly walked his dog here during a royal visit in 1685. The Parks occupy about 70 acres in all and are a wonderful combination of arboretum, river walk and sports ground as well as an available space for Oxford University to hold outdoor celebrations, such as the schoolchildren's tea in 1897 on the occasion of Queen Victoria's Golden Jubilee and for various coronations and jubilees ever since. During the First World War troops drilled in the Parks and even erected aeroplane hangars and a military camp. In the Second World War, they just planted vegetables and dug an air raid shelter under the cricket pavilion.

From the High Bridge turn left towards the centre of the Parks and continue past the Cricket Pavilion, heading left for the Keble gate to return to the centre of town along Parks Road. Call in at The King's Arms for refreshments.

For more information about Headington, go to www.headington.org.uk. For more details about the trees and plants in the University Parks, go to www.parks.ox.ac.uk/guide

*O rest a bit for tis a rare place to rest at.

Woodstock and Blenheim Palace

WALK 15

This walk explores the delightful town of Woodstock, an area frequented by England's monarchs from at least the 10th century and once home to a thriving glove-making industry. It also affords breathtaking views of Blenheim Palace, the Duke of Marlborough's reward for his famous victories against the French and Winston Churchill's birthplace, an architectural masterpiece by Vanburgh set in Capability Brown's park with its magnificent lake.

Start	Finish	Distance	Refreshments
Marlborough Arms, Woodstock	The Museum of Oxfordshire	4 miles (6.3 kms)	Hampers

Blenheim Palace

ON THIS WALK

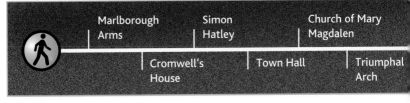

Marlborough Arms — Simon Hatley — Church of Mary Magdalen

Cromwell's House — Town Hall — Triumphal Arch

If you come by car, park on Park Street or in the car park on Hensington Road (first on the right as you enter Woodstock). Otherwise, take the S3 bus from the Central Bus Station in Oxford and get out on Oxford Road, opposite the Marlborough Arms, the walk's starting point.

You are now in Woodstock, the 'clearing in the woods' where the Norman kings enthusiastically established a royal hunting forest and which grew into the town of today because the royal retinue needed somewhere to stay. **The Marlborough Arms** began life as a 14th century coaching inn and you can still see the archway where the coaches used to enter. Note also the old coach lamps either side of the entrance.

To the right of the pub, on the corner of Hensington Road, notice the imposing Vanburgh-style **Hope House**, dating from 1720, behind which the Pullens Glove Factory used to operate.

Walk past Hope House and turn right into High Street, past the **Crown Inn** on your right, another of the old coaching inns of Woodstock and testament to the busy traffic in and out of the town over the centuries. It dates back to the 15th century.

Now cross over High Street to find **Cromwell's House** on the left at No. 28 with its attractive canopy

over the front door and small bronze relief of Oliver Cromwell, head of the Parliamentarians, who apparently stayed here during the Civil War when his forces were besieging Woodstock Manor. After a month, the King's men finally ran out of ammunition and surrendered. The Royalist bastion of Woodstock had fallen. King Charles I himself had stayed here before the war in 1643 to avoid an outbreak of plague in London.

Continue across Park Lane to No. 20 High Street. Beside the door find the name 'Ye Anciente House' and look at the elaborately carved fascia and the canopy with its brackets. Also notice that the house still possesses its late 18th century plaque above the door showing that it was insured with Sun Insurance. The house dates from 1627 and the huge timbers around the door are reputed to come from captured galleons of the Spanish Armada.

Walk on to No.6 and see the plaque to **Simon Hatley**, the inspiration for Samuel Taylor Coleridge's poem *The Rime of the Ancient Mariner*. It was he who shot the albatross, 'the bird that made the breeze to blow', and brought disaster on himself and his ship. He was born in Woodstock in 1685.

Farther down High Street, is the impressive building of **Woodstock Town Hall**, commissioned by the 4th Duke of Marlborough from Sir William Chambers in 1766, made of Cotswold

Blenheim Park		Blenheim Palace		Glover House	
	Column of Victory		Fair Rosamund's Well		Museum of Oxfordshire

limestone and standing on the site of the former Market Cross (whose sundial is inscribed 'Tempus Fugit') and the Penniless Bench where the poor used to sit hoping for some charity. The ground floor remained an open market area until the end of the 19th century.

Just beyond the Town Hall you will come to the **Bear Hotel**, another original coaching inn which claims to have already been 450 years old when Queen Anne gave the Royal Manor of Woodstock to the Duke of Marlborough in 1704, though the oldest buildings here are 17th century and part of the hotel occupies the site of a former glove factory.

At this point, Market Street and High Street merge to become Park Street. Farther on to your left is the church of **Mary Magdalene**, of which the oldest features are a Norman doorway with chevrons to the ground and 13th century windows. If you arrive on the hour, you may also hear the musical clock playing a tune.

Note the blue plaque on the wall of No.5 ahead of you, commemorating Edmund Hiorne, Town Clerk at the time of the Civil War, a Royalist humiliated by the Parliamentarians by being forced to kneel in the House of Commons to beg forgiveness for giving Woodstock's town armour to the forces of the King. He was later reinstated on the accession of Charles II.

Across the road, in front of **The Museum of Oxfordshire**, you can see the original town stocks, where people were trapped by the legs as punishment for minor offences. They have five holes because misdemeanours merited either one or two leg punishments, depending

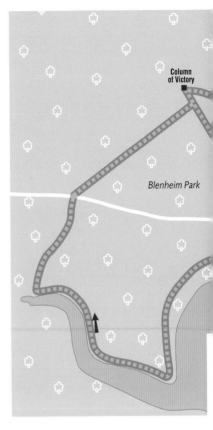

Column of Victory

Blenheim Park

on whether they had affected anyone else, so at least three people could be held at the same time. There used also to be a ducking stool here.

Continue to the end of Park Street, passing Chaucer's House on your right, which apparently once belonged to Chaucer's son, Geoffrey and turn left at the corner to see the **Triumphal Arch**, designed by the architect Hawksmoor and commissioned by Sarah Churchill, wife of the Duke of Marlborough, as a testament to her love and admiration for him. There is a touching inscription on the inside but you need to buy a ticket to see it.

Retrace your steps and turn left down Chaucer Lane, continuing

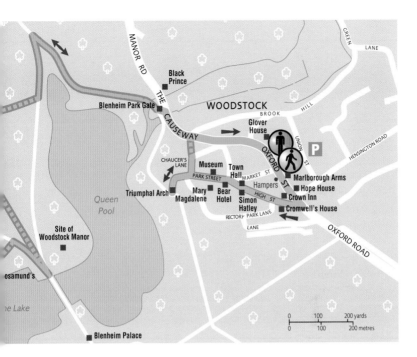

down the Hoggrove Hill steps directly in front of you rather than following the road to the right. At the bottom of the steps, turn left along the Causeway and walk along until you reach a green door with the number 95 on it. Pause to look across the River Glyme to the **Black Prince** pub, so called because Edward the Black Prince, eldest son of Edward III, was born just behind it in 1330.

Go through the gate and find another gate on your left admitting you to **Blenheim Park**. On entering the park turn right and notice the country's first park wall running alongside. Henry I first erected a seven-mile long wall around the park in 1100, expelling the residents to live in the town, and kept a menagerie here, complete with lions, leopards, camels and a porcupine. Interestingly, much later the park was home to a tiger, the property of the

4th Duke of Marlborough, who was given it by Clive of India. If you get a chance to tour the Private Apartments of Blenheim Palace, you can see a magnificent Stubbs painting of the animal in the current Duke's sitting room.

Continue towards the end of the lake and then follow the path round to the left. On your right, opposite the lakeside (here known as the Queen Pool), climb over the stile and head up to the **Column of Victory** topped by a figure of the 1st Duke of Marlborough dressed as a Roman Centurion. This is the ultimate monument to Marlborough's victory over the previously unbeaten Louis XIV of France at the Battle of Blenheim during the War of the Spanish Succession, but it also celebrates numerous other triumphs over the French and the Bavarians. Indeed, the four sides of the pediment of the column are crammed with almost unreadable text, detailing all the Duke's battles and also eulogising Marlborough's sovereign, Queen Anne, to whom Marlborough's wife, Sarah Churchill, was lady-in-waiting and a great friend until they fell out in later life. Queen Anne initially promised Blenheim to Marlborough but later refused to pay for all of it, winning a law case against the Marlboroughs because Godolphin, the Lord Treasurer, had omitted to put the Queen's promise in writing.

Look back to see a fantastic view of **Blenheim Palace** laid out before you. The architect Vanburgh was responsible for designing it, though he eventually parted company with the Marlboroughs having spent £240,000 on completing just a third of it (for comparison, the whole of Castle Howard cost £50,000) and having completely exasperated the Duke's wife, Sarah Churchill, who was trying to keep control of the finances. It was completed by Hawksmoor and certainly repays close inspection, so it is worth buying an entrance ticket and taking a look around. The outside of the palace is covered in military regalia and triumphal symbols – armour, cannon balls, British lions crushing French cockerels... and the inside is truly spectacular. The furniture and the tapestries are beautiful, the portraits (particularly if you listen to one of the guides) are fascinating, there are various collections of porcelain – in particular a Meissen set swapped with King Augustus III of Poland by the 3rd Duke of Marlborough for a pack of hunting dogs (who unfortunately all turned out to be male and not to respond to Polish or German commands). There is also a permanent Winston Churchill exhibition and an automated tour called 'The Untold Story', not to mention a

fabulous café on the water terrace. Note also that your ticket gives you access to the pleasure gardens and the rest of the park, where you can find the Temple of Artemis, Winston Churchill's chosen location for his proposal to his beloved Clementine.

If you do go to the palace, notice the Marlboroughs' eccentric family motto 'Fiel pero Desdichado' (Loyal but Unfortunate) which is proudly emblazoned on the impressive side entrance gate. It originates from the 1st Duke's father, a loyal Royalist who lost everything but his head to the Parliamentarians in the Civil War.

Go down the hill towards the palace and through the gate before the bridge. To your left is the site of the original **Woodstock Manor**, where Elizabeth I was imprisoned for a year in 1554 by her sister Mary Tudor (or 'Bloody' Mary) after the Wyatt uprising. After the Civil War siege referred to earlier in the walk, the house was left a ruin, though Vanburgh did later secretly spend some of the Marlboroughs' money doing it up and living there himself, after which Sarah Churchill had it pulled down.

Now turn right, back up the road and then take the path on the left 50 yards farther on. This affords you a closer look at the lake, created by Capability Brown's damming of the River Glyme, and the beautiful lakeside cedars of Lebanon and bulrushes. In about 50 yards you will find the 'Harry Potter Tree' where Snape was bullied by being dangled upside down by James Potter in the film *The Order of the Phoenix*. A few yards further on find **Fair Rosamund's Well** on the right, now looking rather forlorn. Rosamund (Jane) Clifford was the mistress of Henry II (see walk 12) and legend has it that the couple had secret trysts in a bower at the centre of a maze, thus avoiding discovery by the Queen (Eleanor of Aquitaine) but the latter tied silk to the King's spur, enabling her to follow him through the maze and poison Rosamund.

Continue along the path up the rise and then down along the lake until you reach its tip, at which point, turn right up a path between two hillocks and you will eventually come back to the road which you turned off to go to Fair Rosamund's Well. Cross over and climb the stile, continuing up past the Column of Victory and retracing your steps to the gate where you entered. Walk back up the causeway and then cross the road to the beginning of Oxford Street.

On your left halfway up the road notice the unusual Octagon House, a converted chapel. Continue up the hill past Glover Mews to reach **Glover House**. This was one of the old glove factories of Woodstock as it tells you on the door, the centre of an industry for which the town was famous for hundreds of years until its final decline in the 1950s. The leather came from the deer in Wychwood Forest on the edge of Woodstock and water from the River Glyme was used in the tanning process. Gloves had huge symbolic as well as practical significance. High ranking clergy wore white gloves when performing the sacraments and judges were presented with them in celebration of a 'maiden' assize (a court session when there were no criminals condemned to death

and thus no blood to be spilled), they were placed in the coffins of kings and presented to honoured guests. Indeed, the Ashmolean Museum in Oxford has a (huge) pair of gloves presented to Queen Elizabeth I on a visit to Woodstock and when Queen Elizabeth II visited the town in 1956 she was also presented with a (much smaller!) pair. If you want to find out more about the glove industry, as well as the decorative steel industry which was once important to the town of Woodstock, head back down Market Street to The Museum of Oxfordshire which is behind the stocks on Park Street. They have a very fine exhibition devoted to the town's history.

If you are in a car, head to Bladon to visit Winston Churchill's grave at St Martin's Church. Cross the road outside the White House pub and follow the sign taking you up the path to the left.

Otherwise, for refreshment call in at Hampers near the bus stop in Oxford Street.

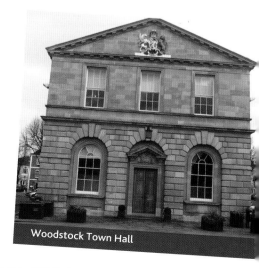
Woodstock Town Hall

For Yehu, light of my life, and all the magic children.

Walks: Devised and written by Victoria Bentata Azaz

Photography: Yehu Azaz. Front cover: Queen's College, © FenlioQ/Shutterstock
with additional images:
Page 26 - Kevin Freeborn
Page 54 - ©iStockphoto.com/Julian Fletcher
Page 56 - ©iStockphoto.com/Andrew Howe
Page 59 - ©iStockphoto.com/Peter Spiro

Maps: Cosmographics Ltd

Design: Ark Creative (UK) Ltd

ISBN: 978-0-31909-117-3

While every care has been taken to check the accuracy and reliability of the
information in this guide, the author and publisher cannot accept responsibility for
errors or omissions or for changes in details given. When walking in Oxford it is
advisable at all times to act with due care and attention, and anyone using this guide
is responsible for their own well-being and safety.

This edition first published in Great Britain 2012 by Crimson Publishing and reprinted
with amendments in 2015 and 2018.

Crimson Publishing, 19-21C Charles Street, Bath, BA1 1HX

www.pathfinderwalks.co.uk

Printed in India by Replika Press Pvt. Ltd. 3/18

A catalogue record for this book is available from the British Library.

Front cover: Queen's College, ©FenlioQ/Shutterstock

Title page: A colourful University gown